CRETE

ARCHEOLOGICAL AND HISTORICAL SITES
SCENERY TRADITIONAL CUSTOMS

ARCHEOLOGICAL AND HISTORICAL MAP OF CRETE

SUPERVISION OF TEXTS

SOSSO LOGIADOU - PLATONOS

ARCHEOLOGIST

ATHENS

ISBN 960-7310-55-1

 COPYRIGHT: D. & I. MATHIOULAKIS
ADDRESS: ANDROMEDAS 1 ATHENS 16231
TEL. 7661351 - 7227229
TRANSLATOR: DAVID HARDY

CRETE

Crete, the fifth largest island in the Mediterranean, lies in the eastern basin of that sea, between Europe, Asia and Africa. Its North coast is washed by the Cretan Ocean and its South by the Libyan Ocean.

The island is long and narrow and has an east-west orientation, tilting somewhat towards the north west Corner. Its surface area is 8.305.7 square kilometres, and it is 257 kilometres long (the road running the lenght of the island is about 400 kilometres) and from 12 to 61 kilometres across. The coastline is 1046 kilometres long. According to the 1991 census, the population of the island is 536,980.

Crete is mainly mountainous, with three large ranges: the White Mountains (Sfakianes Madares), 2453 m. high, the legendary Ida (Psiloriti), 2456 m. high. and Dikte, 2148 m. high. The mountains are split by deep, wild gorges, the most famous of which is the gorge of Samaria in the White Mountains. This is 18 kilometres long and 600 m. deep in many places.

The island has few plains: the largest of them are those of **Kissamos, Kydonia, Apokorona, Rethymnon-Mylopotamos, Ai Vassilios, Heraklion, Messara** and **Ierapetra**. There are, however, many mountain plateaux (amongst which are those of **Omalos** and **Lassithi**) and a large number of valleys.

The Cretan rivers are not large; amongst them are the **Platanias**, the **Kladissos**, the **Yeropotamos**, the **Anapodaris** and the three **Almyri**.

The most important bays in Crete are those of **Kissamos, Chania, Souda, Almyros, Messara, Heraklion, Malia, Merambello** and **Sitia**.

The main natural harbours are at **Souda, Poros (Elounda)** and **Ayios Nikolaos.**

There are a large number of barren islands off the coasts of Crete. **Gramboussa, Thodorou** or **Ai Theodoroi, Ayioi Pantes, Dia, Spinalonga, Pseira, Dionyssades, Elassa, Grandes, Koufonissi, Khryssi (Gaidouronissi), Paximadia, Gavdos.**

It has been asserted that Gavdos is the **Ogygia** of legend, the island of **Kalypso.** It has even been claimed that in the island is the site of the cave in which the much-sung Nymph kept Odysseus close to her for seven years.

The islands of Ayioi Theodoroi, Dia and Ayioi Pantes are nowadays grazing grounds for the famous Cretan chamois (kri-kri), which are the only ones of their kind in the world.

Crete is divided for administrative purposes into four departments — those of **Chania, Rethymnon, Heraklion** and **Lassithi** — with 20 provinces 11 demi, 570 communities and 1447 villages. Communication with mainland Greece is by boat or air, and there are daily departures from Piraeus or from the Hellenikon airport. The distance from Piraeus to Heraklion is 175 miles and to Souda (Chania) 156 miles.

The boats in service on the Cretan line today are quick, comfortable luxury FERRY BOATS.

The boat journey takes about ten hours, while the plane takes about 30 minutes.

The soil of Crete is generally speaking fertile, and its produce is renowned for its quality and flavour. The main products are oil, cereals, chestnuts, cherries, almonds and walnuts, raisins (sultanina), fresh grapes (the famous "rozaki"), excellent wines and select cheeses, like the well known graviera. During recent years the cultivation of early garden produce — mainly tomatoes — and flowers has spread, with good results. Pliny's statement that whatever is produced on this island is incomparably better than similar products from other places is indicative of the richness of the Cretan flora.

The climate is gentle and mild, and is described as temperate, marine and mediterranean. As a climatic area, Crete as a whole is the no-man's land between the temperate and the tropical climatic zones.

The French traveller **Savary** thought it was the best and healthiest climate in the world. **Hippokrates,** the father of medicine, recommended it to anyone recovering from illness. **Theophrastos,** the father of botany, described Crete as 'rich in medicines' because of its important plants.

The most important of these is dittany, (diktamon), which has marvellous properties. In his work concerning the history of animals Aris-

4

totle claims that the Cretan chamois eats dittany leaves when it is wounded to make the arrow fall out.

Many ancient authors dealt with the flora of Crete, and modern writers, too, refer to or describe a large number of Cretan plants in their works. It may be said that the Cretan flora has been more studied than that of any other part of the world.

The geographical position of Crete, the great variety of its terrain, its rich flora and other factors condueive to animal life have created generally favourable conditions for the development of a very varied animal life, very similar to that of other mediterranean countries. Crete has many names in the ancient authors:

Aeria, from its temperate climate,

Chthonia, from Demeter who was worshipped as a chthonic deity in Crete.

Doliche, from its long narrow shape.

Telchinia, from the Telchines, or metal working gods.

Idaia, from Mount Ida, or from the nymph Idaia.

Makaris, as the country of the blessed.

Kouretis, as the country of the Kouretes, and

Crete, from the nymph Krete of from Kres the son of Zeus, who was its ancient king.

Crete appears to have been first inhabited during the Neolithic period — that is from the 6th millenium B.C. The earliest inhabitants may have come from Asia Minor. Their culture was still relatively primitive, but it had reached the stage of production, involving the cultivation of the soil and the keeping of domesticated animals. They knew how to make fine burnished pottery, frequently decorated with incised geometric motifs, and were capable of building stone houses, though they also still made use of caves for habitation. Metals were as yet unknown and the tools and weapons they needed (hammers, axes, knives etc.) were made of a range of hard stones, and obsidian from Melos. The simple, relatively primitive figurines suggest that they worshipped a female fertility goddess.

The Neolithic was followed by the Bronze Age civilisation which the English archaeologist **Arthur Evans,** who excavated the palace at knossos, called "Minoan" after **Minos,** the legendary king of Crete. This civilisation lasted over 1500 years, from 2600-1100 B.C., and reached the height of its prosperity in the 18th-16th centuries.

Very little was known about Minoan Crete before the great excavations of Greek and foreign archaeologists that began about 1900, and the discovery of the palaces of Knossos and Phaestos, with their astonishing architecture and wonderful finds. Its history had passed into the realm of legend and remained a distant memory in Greek tradition and mythology. The ancient authors speak mainly of Minos, the king who had his capital at Knossos, and was a wise lawgiver, a fair judge (who therefore judged souls in Hades after his death, along with Rhadamanthys and Aiakos) and a great sea-dominator. Homer calls him «companion of mighty Zeus", and Thucydides informs us that he was the first man to hold sway over the Aegean with his fleet, and that he captured and colonised the Cyklades, driving out the Carians, and freeing the seas from piracy. Plato speaks of the heavy tribute that the inhabitants of Attica were compelled to pay to Minos — the historical basis of the myth of Theseus can easily be recognised — and Aristotle attributes his thalassocracy to the geographical position of Crete.

This position was, in fact, particularly favourable, both for the Minoan domination of the sea, and for the growth and development of their wonderful civilisation. It was the crossroads linking three continents, and the racial elements and cultural strands of Asia, Africa and Europe met and mingled here to produce a new way of life, a new philosophy of the world and an exceptionally fine art that still strikes one today with its freshness, charm, variety, and mobility.

The mixture of racial elements in Crete is demonstrated by the different skull-types discovered in the excavations there. In general terms, however, the Minoans form part of the so-called "Mediterranean type": they were of medium height and had black curly hair and

Minoan Types

brown eyes.Their language is not known, for the written texts have not yet been deciphered, but it appears to have belonged to a separate category of the Mediterranean languages. After 1450 B.C. when the Achaeans had established themselves in Crete, a very archaic form of Greek was used as the official language and gained some dissemination. This is the language that may be read in the Linear B texts deciphered by VENTRIS. The earlier Minoan language was still spoken alongside it by the Eteocretans ("the true Cretans"); this fact is attested by Eteocretan inscriptions discovered in East Crete, dating from the 6th and 5th centuries B.C.

Homer was aware that the inhabitants of Crete were divided into a number of tribes, and mentions the names of five of them: the Pelasgians, the Eteocretans, the Kydonians, the Achaeans and the Dorians, adding that each spoke its own language. He also emphasizes how densely populated Crete was, with its ninety cities, and mentions some of them, such as Knossos, Phaestos, Gortys, Lyttos, Kydonia, and Rhytion.

Excavation has demonstrated the truth of Homer's comments, revealing a host of Minoan sites, four of which were «palace» centres, developing around a large palace. Those known today, apart from Knossos and Phaestos, are at Malia and Zakros.

Evans divided the Minoan age chronologically, on the basis of the pottery, into "Early Minoan", "Middle Minoan" and "Late Minoan". Nowadays a different system of chronology has won general acceptance. It was proposed by Professor N. Platon, and is based upon the great destructions and the life of the Minoan palaces. It gives us the following periods for prehistoric Crete:

Neolithic period	**(6000-2600 B.C.)**
Minoan period	
Pre-palace period:	2600-1900 B.C.
First palace period:	1900-1700 B.C.
Second palace period:	1700-1350 B.C.
Post-palace period:	1350-1100 B.C.
Sub-Minoan period:	1100-1000 B.C.

The Pre-palace period (2600-1900 B.C.) With the arrival of new racial elements in Crete, bronze was used for the first time in the fabrication of tools and weapons. Its use quickly became widespread and continued to the end of the Minoan period. Not enough is known about the pre-palace settlements, but we do know that there were strongly built houses of stone and brick which had large numbers of rooms, paved courtyards and, often, red plaster on the walls. The most typical of them were discovered at Vassiliki and Myrtos (Ierapetra). By way of contrast, the tomps of the period are very well known; there are large vaulted tombs (plain of the Messara), cist tombs cut rock inphelten (Mokhlos), chamber tombs (Agia Photia, Sitia) and grave compounds (Archanes, Khryssolakkos (Malia), Palaikastro, Zakros etc.) The wealth of finds in these tombs supplies us with information about the art and evolution of the pre-palace civilisation.

The pottery has a variety of main styles, known today by the names of Pyrgos, Ag. Onoufrios, Levina, Koumassa and Vassiliki. They are imitations of vessels made of straw, wood or hide and have incised, motifs full of movement painted and mottled decoration. Particularly fine examples are the Vassiliki style pots with their striking mottled decoration, produced by the firing, and their sophisticated shapes, like the "teapot" and the tall, beaked pitchers. The first polychrome pottery makes its appearance towards the end of the period.

7

In the field of miniature art, the gold ware is outstanding (jewellery from Mokhlos and the vaulted tombs of the Messara), as are the excellent, early examples of sealstones made of ivory and steatite.

Society seems to have been organised in genos, or 'clans', and farming, stock-raising, shipping and commerce were developed to a systematic level. The main forms of deity, and the most important cult symbols, had made their appearance in the sphere of religion, figurines of the Mother Goddess being typical.

At the beginning of the **First Palace period (1900-1700 B.C.)**, power began to be centred in the hands of kings, for some unknown reason, and the first large palace centres which had a wide cultural influence in the vital region around them, came into being. Excavation has revealed four large palaces, at Knossos, Phaestos, Malia and Zakros, but there must have been others. It is clear from the scant remains of them that have been discovered beneath the later palaces that they possessed all the features of the fully developed Minoan architecture: the arrangement of the buildings around a central court, the fine façades of closely fitted blocks of poros stone, the large numbers of magazines, the sacred rooms, the different levels and storeys connected by small staircases, and the monumental entrances. The finest example is that uncovered in the west palace section at Phaestos. The most decorative style of pottery in

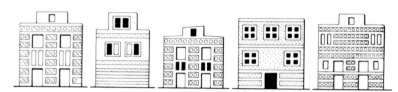

Types of Minoan Houses (Faience)

the world was created in the palace workshops: the Kamares ware, named after the cave of Kamares where it was first discovered. Its motifs are polychrome and full of movement; they are mainly rosettes, spirals and hatching, painted on a shiny black background, and they are found on a variety of vase shapes, made with an astonishing technical perfection. The specialist workshops of the palaces also produced very fine vases or vessels of stone and faience; sealstones of precious or semi-precious stones, with hieroglyphics and dynamic scenes that are often naturalistic; solid elegant weapons and tools; vessels of bronze or silver; jewellery of marvelous technique (the "Pendant of the bees" from Chryssolakkos, Malia is famous) and charming miniature sculpture.

Protopalatial terra-cottas are best known, however, from dedications in the Peak Sanctuaries (cult areas on the peaks of hills or mountains), which are typical of the period. The best known of those discovered so far come from Petsofa, Piskokefalo, Youktas, Kalo Khorio, Kofinas, Traostalos, and Vryssinas. The Minoan pantheon always has the mother goddess as its main element, and the use of sacred symbols (the sacred horns and the double axe) becomes general. Society was organised hierarchically, there was specialisation of labour and contacts with the outside world became more frequent. In the palace archives, use was made of the hieroglyphic script, which quickly developed into a linear one.

A terrible disaster, perhaps caused by earthquakes, reduced the first palace centres and the settlements of Crete to ruins, about 1700 B.C.

During the **Second Palace period (1700-1350 B.C.),** Minoan civilisation reached its zenith. The new palaces that were built upon the ruins of the old ones were much more magnificent; the cities around them expanded and hummed with life; large numbers of rural villas, the residences of local governors, controlled great areas in the same way as the feudal towers of the Middle Ages; the roads increased in number and quality; the harbours were organized, and swift ships carried the products of farming and of Cretan art to the whole of the then civilized world, where they were exchanged for raw materials. The new palaces were multi-storeyed and invariably very complex. They had great courtyards, imposing or picturesque porticoes, broad easy staircases, processional paths and monumental entrances. The royal living quarters had tiers of doors (Polythyra), thrones and benches, as well as bathrooms and interior light wells, and there were rows of sacred quarters and magazines, crypts, and halls for audiences, banquet and sacred ceremonies Finally, there were ancillary areas of all kinds, including workshops, and a water-supply and drainage system based on very ingenuous principles. It is not surprising that buildings as large and complicated as this (the palace at Knossos covers 22.000 square metres and had over 1500 rooms) led the Greek imagination to create the myth of the labyrinth. The great palaces had one feature in common with the smaller ones, that were perhaps the summer residences of the kings (like those at Knossós, Archanes and Agia Triada near Phaestos): this was the wonderful fresco painting decorating the walls with fresh, lively scenes in an array of colours, or the dazzling white and veined blocks of gupsum that were used to cover the walls and floors.

The megara, or rural villas of the local governors, at Vathypetro, Sklavokambos, Tylissos, Metropolis (Gortys), Nirou Khani, Zou, Pyrgos

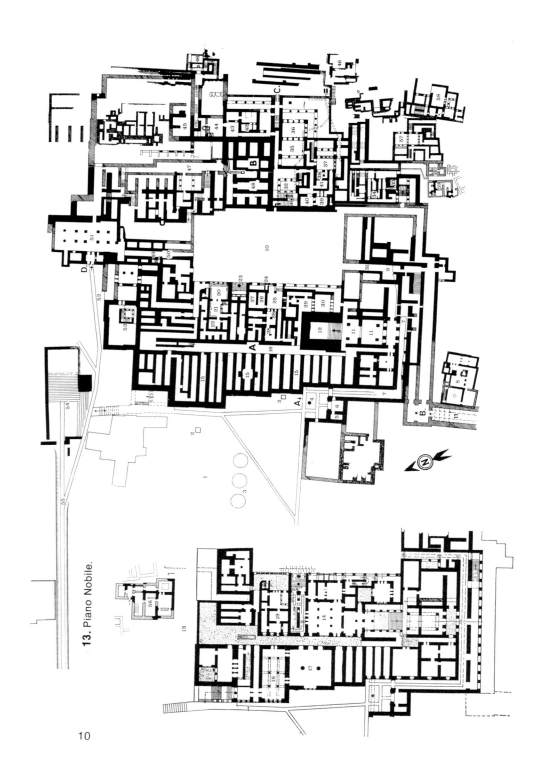

13. Piano Nobile.

10

PLAN OF THE PALACE OF MINOS AT KNOSSOS

A west wing.

B east wing.

A. West Entrance.
B. South Entrance.

C. East Entrance.
D. North Entrance.

1. West Court.
2. Altars.
3. Sacred Waste Pits, ('Koulouras').
4. West Porch.
5. Gate-keeper's Lodge.
6. Room with Throne.
7. Corridor of the Procession.
8. South House.
9. Corridor to the Central Court.
10. Central Court.
11. South Propylaeum.
12. Staircase.
13. Piano Nobile.
14. Tri-Columnar Shrine.
15. West Magazines.
16. Corridor of the Magazines.
17. Great Hall.
18. Room of the Shrine.
19. Rooms with copies of frescoes.
20. Anteroom to the Throne Room.

21. Throne Room.
22. Interior Shrine.
23. Central Staircase.
24. Tri-partite Shrine.
25. Anteroom of the Pillar Crypts.
26. Room of the Tall Pithos.
27. Temple Repositories.
28. Square-Pillar Crypts.
29. Area of the "Chariot Tablets".
30. "Temple of Rhea".
31. The Prince with the Lilies.
32. Grand Staircase.
33. Shrine of the Double Axes.
34. Lustral Basin.
35. Hall of the Double Axes or
36. King's Megaron.
37. Queen's Megaron.
38. Queen's Bathroom.
39. Queen's Toilet Room.
40. Court of the Distaffs.

41. Treasury.
42. Lapidary's Workshop.
43. Potter's Workshop.
44. Court of the Stone Spout.
45. Magazines of the Giant Pithoi.
46. East Bastion.
47. Corridor of the Draught Board.
48. Magazine of the Pithoi with Medallions.
49. Bastion of the N. Entrance.
50. Passage of the N. Entrance.
51. Custom House.
52. NW Entrance.
53. Lustral Basin.
54. Theatre.
55. Royal Road.
56. House of the Frescoes.
57. House of the Chancel Screen.
58. SE House.
59. House of the Sacrified Oxen.
60. House of the Fallen Blocks.

(Myrtos). Praessos. Apano Zakros and elsewhere, had a farming and industrial character, emerging clearly from the interesting buildings that survive.

The social system was probably feudal and theocratic, and the king of each palace centre was also the supreme religious leader. There may have been a hierarchy of these priest-kings, headed by the ruler of Knossos. Thanks to this system, continuous peace — the famous **PAX MINOICA** — prevailed throughout the island, which facilitated the great cultural development, the charming, refined way of life, and the Cretan thalassocracy.

The art of the second palaces is naturalistie for the most part, and demonstrates the love of the Minoans for eternal, all-powerful and constantly renewed nature, as well as its internal, spiritual counter Part.

A variety of pottery styles developed: the marine style, with its lively motifs derived from the varied and striking world of the deep (octopuses, tritons, star-fishes, sea-snails, rocks, seaweed etc.); the floral style, with its fresh plants and open flowers; the decorated style, the basic motif of which is the spiral in a variety of complicated arrangements, though it also has sacred symbols and weapons; and, during the final phase of the period, the "palace" style, with its tectonic forms and decoration arranged in bands.

The fresco — a particular feature of the period — was used on a much greater scale than previously to decorate the palaces and wealthy houses. Landscapes were now depicted (royal gardens with exotic animals, such as monkeys, thickets of dense vegetation, birds, wild cats and deer), and there are scenes from cult and from social life: scenes of festival occasions in the palaces and sanctuaries (the miniature frescoes from Knossos,) of contests such as bull-leaping, held in honour of the deity, and of ritual, such as the "holy Communion" with the Parisienne. The relief fresco was used to portray majestic figures of princes and high priests (Prince with the Lilies) and sacred or imaginary animals (bulls, sphinxes, griffins etc.).

In the field of plastic art, the figures were more natural and complete, like the fifurines with the beautiful hairstyles from Piskokefalo (Sitia), and the plastic rhytons in the shapes of bulls or wild cats. The stone vases and vessels were made of fine veined, coloured stone or of rare, hard stones, alabaster, marble, rock crystal, obsidian, porphyry and basalt. They often take the form of sacred animals or animal heads, like the superb bulls' heads from Knossos and Zakros; or they may be decorated with masterful relief scenes like the ones from Agia Triada (harvesters rhyton, rhyton of the sacred games, cup of the report) and the rhyton with the peak sanctuary, from Zakros.

Faience was used for the working of rare, luxury items such as plastic rhytons (Zakros), decorative or votive plaques (the "town mosaic", and votive reliefs from Knossos), and unique figurines like the snake goddesses. There are works of a similar technical perfection in gold and ivory, such as the chrysselephantine bull-leaper from Knossos; royal gaming boards; gold rings engraved with miniature scenes of ritual, that afford so much information about Minoan religion; a wide range of jewellery; and vessels either made of gold or silver, or gilded. The handles of the long swords or elegant daggers of this period often have a gold covering and gold nails.

In addition to bronze weapons and tools of all kinds, many of which are like those of the present day, there are some very fine bronze vessels with carefully worked and graceful repoussée decoration.

The sealstones of the second palace period are made of precious and semi-precious stones, and represent wonderfully natural scenes from the animal world and from the religious cycle. They are usually lentoid or almond-shaped.

The main deity is always the Mother Goddess, who is portrayed in her different forms. She is the chthonic goddess with the snakes, the "Ministress of the Animals" with lions and chamois, and the goddess of the heavens, with birds and stars. The powerful god of fertility was worshipped together with her, apparently in the form of a bull, as were the young couple, boy and girl, who died or were lost in the autumn and came back to the light and life in the spring, thus representing the cycle of nature. Alongside them there existed a whole exotic world of monstrous demons to serve them, and facilitate communications between man and the divinity.

The deities were worshipped in sanctuaries in the palaces, houses or countryside, in the peak sanctuaries and in sacred caves. Many of the features of Minoan religion passed into the cycle of Greek mystery religions. Most of the tombs were cut into the soft rock and had a square burial chamber and a sloping dromos. Some were still vaulted tombs with a circular or rectangular chamber.

The south royal tomb-sanctuary at Knossos consists of a complete building complex, with a small portico, a crypt with a sacred Pillar, a chamber cut into the rock, and an upper floor for the cult of the dead. It is very reminiscent of the "tomb of Minos" in Sicily described by Diodoros.

The hieroglyphic script of the preceding period now developed into Linear A. The surviving texts — there are about two hundred — are written in the unknown Minoan language on clay "tablets", and appear to contain information relating to accounts. They come from the archives of palaces or villas (Knossos, Archanes, Tylissos, Agia Triada, Phaestos, Zakros, Chania). The "Phaestos Disk", with its unique hieroglyphic text, belongs to the first phase of the second palace period. The hieroglyphic script seems to have survived from earlier times and to have' been used by the priests to write religious texts.

About 1450, all the centres of the second palace period were destroyed by the terrible volcanic eruption of Santorini. Life was resumed only in the palace at Knossos, which was reconstructed and served as the residence of a new Achaean dynasty. The presence of this dynasty is attested both by the very archaic Greek language written in Linear B and by the appearance of the "Palace Style" pottery. Many changes were made in the arrangement of the palaces, and it is to this period that the "throne room" belongs, as does the final form and decoration (with frescoes) of the "Corridor of the Procession", and most of the other surviving frescoes.

Post-palace period (1350-1100 B.C.)

After the final destruction of about 1350, none of the Minoan palaces was re-inhabited. The Achaeans built their simple Mycenean megara on other sites, as yet unknown; remains of these have survived only over the ruins of earlier royal villas (as Agia Triada), and farms or houses (as Tylissos). Not even the palace of Idomeneus, the king of Knossos who took part in the Trojan War with his friend Meriones and 80 ships, has been discovered. A great number of Mycenean centres are known, however; these now spread throughout the whole of Crete, and most of them existed down into Greek times (Kydonia, Polyrrhenia, Kissamos, Knossos, Cortys, Phaestos, Lyktos, Arkadia, Rhytion etc.)

The basis of the new civilisation was Minoan, but its spirit was archaic Greek, and it showed a tendency towards an architectural structure and uniformity. The labyrinthine buildings were replaced by the austere Mycenean megaron; the predominant pottery style was the so-called "Mycenean koine", in which the same shapes were continually repeated, with simple decoration. and the frescoes lost their former freedom and vigour. In the sphere of plastic clay art, there were large, impressive clay figurines, but even these were schematic and rigid (Metropolis (Gortys), Gournia, Gazi).

There was no substantial change in religion or cult. The tombs were mainly chamber tombs with a long dromos, as before, but the grave foods are poorer, and most of the jewels accompanying the dead were made of coloured glass paste.

The last phase of this period was a time of decline and disorder caused by the movement of the "Sea Peoples" in the East Mediterranean. The forerunners of the Dorians seem to have begun to arrive in Crete, for a number of new cultural features make their appearance in sporadic fashion: cremation of the dead, for example, iron weapons and tools, brooches - which attest a new style of dress - and geometric decorative motifs.

Crete entered upon the purely Greek period of its history with the arrival of massive waves of Dorians, about 1100 B.C. The **Protogeometric period** that followed **(1100-900 B.C.)** unfolded alongside the **Sub-Minoan,** for the earlier Cretan cultural tradition continued to offer resistance in certain areas, particularly the mountain centres of the Eteocretans in central and eastern Crete (Karfi (Lassithi), Vrokastro (Merambello), Praessos and other places near Sitia), and to exercise some influence on the uncouth conquerors. No one today doubts the contribution made by the Minoan and Mycenean civilisations to the creation of the Greek miracle.

The use of iron, and cremation of the dead became general, and the urns for the ashes are amongst the most characteristic vessels of the period. The finest examples of them come from Fortetsa, near Knossos, and some of them reveal the influence of Athens on the protogeometric art of Crete.

Geometric and Orientalizing periods (900-600 B.C.)

The geometric period saw the foundation of the citystates of Dorian Crete, which numbered about 150, judging by the names of them preserved in the ancient authors. Most of them claimed to have been founded by a Greek hero, or a descendant of heroes. Many of them, however, like Lato, Rhizenia, Dreros and Axos, simply developed hom Achaean-Sub-Minoan settlements. Herodotos claims that Lyttos was the first city to be settled by the Dorians, but its name demonstrates that it was of Minoan origin. Over half of the cities mentioned in the ancient authorities have so far been identified, the most famous and most important of them being Knossos, Phaestos, Gortys, Lyttos, Chersonessos, Rhizenia, Bienna (Biannos), in Central Crete, Axos, Eleutherna, Lappa, Aptera, Kissamos, Elyros, Lissos, Polyrrhenia, all in Western Crete, and Milatos, Dreros, Lato, Olous, Hierapytna, Praessos, Itanos, Seteia, and Ampelos, in Eastern Crete.

The constitution of Dorian Crete was similar to that of the Spartans, though many of the earlier written laws were still observed, particularly by the subject population. Tradition has it that Lykourgos, the Spartan lawgiver, derived his laws from Crete many of the provisions of Cretan law are known from the famous archaic inscription from Gortys, which dates from the beginning of the 5th century B.C.

The pre-Greek inhabitants of Crete were divided into three classes, according to the strength of their resistance to the conqueror: the "perioikoi", whose position was better than that of their counterparts in other Dorian areas, the Minoans, who were slaves cultivating public land, and the "Aphamiotes" or "Klarotes", who were slaves working on private land. Class divisions also existed amongst the conquerors. The elite consisted of the "hippeis", from amongst whom were chosen the ten "kosmoi" - the highest officials of the state, who exercised absolute authority.

The members of the "gerousia", who exercised administrative and judicial authority, were all former kosmoi. It was only in the "ekklessia tou demou", a body with no important powers, that all the free citizens took part.

The education of the citizen was organized along military lines, as at Sparta, and began at eighteen. At this age, the "epheboi" had to leave their homes and become members of an "agela" (an education group), where they lived together with their peers under the guidance of a leader until they became men. They were taught the art of war, were trained in running and dancing (the pyrrhikios), learned music, and finally, were "kidnapped" and taken to the mountains by a mature man - the "philetor" - and stayed there for about three months, devoting themselves to hunting.

This frugal, controlled life-style and the austere Doric customs survived in Crete until a relatively late date. Plato, in his "Laws", cites Lyttos as a model of the Dorian constitution, where even the practice of rhetoric was forbidden, since it stood in opposition to their simple, fair concept of life.

The geometric art of Crete, however, lost its severity under the influence of eastern work and of Minoan survivals. These influences are very clear in the wealth of pottery yielded by geometric tombs, particularly those of Fortetsa (Knossos) and Arkades (modern Afrati). In addition to decorative motifs foreign to geometric art, such as the "Tree of Life", mythological scenes (Theseus and Ariadne, a goddess taming large birds etc.) occur for the first time on vases. The splendid examples of metal-work, too, such as the bronze shields and the tympanum from the Idaean Cave, have exotic granulated representations: groups of lions, complex scenes of warfare and hunting, and so on. Gold work still used the wonderful techniques of the earlier period, though the compositions are somewhat inferior (jewels from Teke, Heraklion). Relations with Egypt were renewed, as is clear from the importing of scarabs and figurines (from the altar of "Zeus Thenatas" at Amnissos, and the cave of Eileithyia at Inatos), and also from Egyptian influences on the Cretan "dedalic" school of large-scale plastic art. The founding of this school is attributed in the tradition to the mythical figure Daidalos.

"Dedalic" art reached its peak in the **archaic period (650-500 B.C.)**, particularly during the early part of it. Amongst its most typical products are the large stone goddesses from Eleutherna and Astritsi (Athena), with their luxuriant hair, rather like a wig, their large features, the covering like a shawl around the shoulders and the tight embroidered belts. The reverent seated goddesses from the inner portal of an archaic temple at Prinias have a different hairdress (they wear a cylindrical polos over top of long curls), but the shawl is the same, as is the belt, and there are embroidered motifs on the dresses.

They are standing on bands of animals carved in relief and clearly represent a continuation of the primeval "Mistress of the Animals", whom we may now call the Cretan Artemis or Britomartis. The frieze with the figures of the proud horsemen also comes from this temple. The Cretan triads carved on large relief slabs or in the form of seated statues, are represented amongst the sculptures from the archaic temple on the acropolis of Gortys. Primitive forms of Greek gods are also to be seen in other stone statues, both large and small, and in ceramic or bronze sphyrelata statues, like those of Apollo, Leto, and Artemis from Dreros. Clay votive tablets from Gortys frequently depict Aphrodite, naked, Athena, and the Cretan triad.

Plastic art is represented by a very interesting series of large pithos jars decorated with bands of wild animals, sphinxes, griffins, snakes, scenes depicting the Mistress of the Animals, and so on.

The engraved funerary stelai from Prinias, with the scenes of warriors, and women who are probably "heroised", represent an art form somewhere between sculpture and painting. The trimmed bronze sheets from Afrati and Symi (the Sanctuary of Hermes Dendrites), with the incised figures of worshippers and mythological scenes are the counterparts of them in the field of metal work. The series of offensive and defensive weapons, mitrai for the protection of the abdomen and helmet from Axos, Cretan breastplate from Olympia) are also wonderful examples of metal work.

This is the final flowering of autonomous Cretan art, however. Aristocratic conservatism, the militaristic spirit and above all the wars that began to be waged between the city-states of Crete led to a swift decline in the culture. Most of the last remaining Cretan artists of any note left the island and worked and taught in artistic centres elsewhere, thus making their contribution to the creation of the Creek miracle.

During the **Classical period,** Crete was cut off from the rest of Greece. It took no part in the Persian wars, and remained neutral during the Peloponnesian war. The cities continued to possess a well-organized administration, with their kosmoi, and continued to implement their lawcodes, with the necessary local adjustments, but strife between cities, or leagues of cities, became widespread, and there was no time for involvement in foreign wars.

Rivalry was fierce, particularly between cities in the same area as each other, which sometimes went to the extreme of totally annihilating their rival. The main protagonists in Central Crete were Knossos, Lyttos, Gortys, and Phaestos. Kydonia often threw her weight into the wars between Knossos and Gortys, sometimes on one side and sometimes on the other. Rhizinia (Prinias) appears finally to have been destroyed during this period; its life came to an end after the archaic period. Relations between Priansos, Itanos and Arkades seem to have been no better. In Eastern Crete, Ierapetra opposed Itanos and Lato Olous. In Western Crete there was a totally destructive war between Kydonia and Apollonia.

Art, naturally enough, did not flourish in this climate. The very few pieces of classical sculpture that survive have a provincial character (metope of Eurystheus from Knossos; funerary stele with a scene of farewell, from Heraklion). A few pieces of excellent quality are clearly imports from Attica or the islands.

Plastic art produced better work (terracottas), found in the Sanctuaries of Demeter and Aphrodite at Knossos, Gortys and Olous, and other sanctuaries or storerooms in East Crete, such as the Dictaean sanctuary at Palaikastro and the stores at Anavlokhos and the Roussa Ekklissia.

The coinage reached an even higher artistic level - a further indication of the rivalry between the city-states and their tendency to exercise economic domination over each other. Many classical Cretan coins are amongst the finest in Greece.

The Hellenistic Period (330-69 B.C.) saw a continuation and intensification of the internal wars. Lyttos was completely destroyed by Knossos, Phaestos by Gortys, and Apollonia by Kydonia. The treaties that survive demonstrate that broad coalitions were formed, and alliances sought with the Greek cities and the Hellenistic kingdoms of the East and Egypt. One such treaty is that between Eumenes II and 29 Cretan city-states (mainly in East Crete), and there is archaeological evidence for the existence of a sizeable Egyptian garrison on the island of Leuke (Koufonissi) off the SE coast of Crete.

The intervention of third parties in the internal affairs of Crete, the alliances formed between them, and the uprooting of populations after capture of their cities were undoubtedly some of the major factors that led large numbers of Cretans to serve as mercenaries in foreign armies. The phenomenon had first appeared before the Peloponnesian War and became widespread in the Hellenistic period. The Cretan soldiers acquired a reputation for daring, swiftness and cunning, and in particular for their skill as archers and slingers, and they were in great demand in all the armies, and even in the invincible Roman legions. Mercenary service, however, had an adverse effect on their character and their dour Dorian habits. Towards the end of the period they went so far as to enter into alliance with the pirates of Cilikia, and to offer them the Cretan harbours as headquarters.

Cretan Hellenistic art was always imitative and provincial. There are considerable architectural remains, particularly at Gortys (where there was a rectangular building on the site of the Odeum), on the acropolis of Praessos (a country villa) and at Phaestos, where there were large numbers of buildings both on the site of the palace and on the slopes of the hill.

Interesting Hellenistic tombs have been discovered in the area of Gortys, Ierapetra, Lassithi and Praessos. The most representative works of sculpture are the marble groups of Niobids from Inatos.

The coins continued the fine classical tradition and achieved even greater variety. Series of tetradrachms of Athenian type were struck in some of the cities, bearing the names of local rulers.

Mention should be made, finally, of the interesting series of inscriptions containing some lengthy texts of the treaties.

Greco-Roman period (69 B.C. - A.D. 330)

The cooperation of the Cretans with the pirates of Cilikia, and their relations with Mithridates of Pontos, the irreconcilable enemy of Rome, proved fateful for the island. Rome had, until then, often acted as mediator in the internal affairs of Crete, and the Romans now had the pretext that they needed to attack. They found the Cretans united for perhaps the first time, in one of the most typical examples of the famous Symbretismus in the face of external danger. The first attack by the Roman fleet was repulsed between Heraklion and the island of Dia. Shortly afterwards, however, in 69 B.C., the consul Quintus Caecilius Metellus succeeded in landing three legions near Kydonia, and captured the island after a fierce struggle that lasted for three years. His victory won him the name "Creticus" and the honour of a triumph in Rome.

Crete now became a Roman province, with the provincial capital at first at Knossos, though it was soon transferred to Gortys, the city that had offered least resistance to the conqueror. Under Augustus, Crete was united with the Cyrenaica for administrative purposes. The

Roman praetor or proconsul governed the province from Gortys, which became so populous that it is now estimated that it had about 300.000 inhabitants. The other cities were governed by an imperial appointee of consular rank; the local officials continued to be elected but acted in a purely honorary capacity. The coins of the "Cretan Coinon" show that there existed some kind of federation of Cretan cities.

The famous **PAX ROMANA** had favourable effects in Crete, as elsewhere. The cities flourished once more and were embellished with fine buildings and statues. The ruins of Gortys are spread far and wide in the plain around it. One can still see today the great Praetorium, the Odeum, the Nymphaia, the thermai, the temple of Isis, and the archaic temple of Pythian Apollo, which was adapted in the Hellenistic period by the addition of a pronaos, and received an apse in Roman times. The new colossal statue of the god, which still retained the Hellenistic head, was erected here, (now in Heraklion Museum).

There were many rich Roman houses at Knossos, such as the "Villa of Dionysos", with fine mosaic floors. Monumental cioterns are preserved at Aptera and at Lyttos, which had been rebuilt; the agora of the last may be seen with a large number of honorific statue bases.

At Lebena and Lissos, near the Libyan ocean in an evocative natural environment amidst mountains and close to springs, which were thought to have healing properties, there were sanctuaries of Asklepios with all the buildings necessary for healing the sick worshippers.

Important Roman cemeteries have been discovered at a number of sites, mainly at Knossos (where there were subterranean built tombs), at Gortys, at Agios Thomas (ancient Pannona), at Matalla, at Ierapetra, at Lissos and at Syia (modern Souyia).

Sculpture produced some very fine series of copies of classical works, like the Doryphoros of Polykleites, the Pothos and the Cnidian Aphrodite of Praxiteles, the "squatting" Aphrodite (Doidalsa type) and the Athena of Pheidias. The female "peplos" figures of the Herakleotis type are also interesting, and there are important series of reliefs and of portraits of Roman emperors.

Byzantine period A. (A.D. 330-824)

Crete was separated from the Cyrenaica and attached to Illyria in A.D. 330. From the time of Theodosius the Great (A.D. 395), however, it was a province of the Eastern Roman Empire, under a governor (consularius) appointed by the emperor. At a later date it was a thema under a Byzantine general.

Christianity began to spread to Crete at a very early date. The apostle Titus, a companion of Paul on his travels, settled at Gortyn and from there organized the church. He established the first "elders" in the most important cities of Crete, and these later became the first Bishops. Gortys continued to be the metropolis of the church in Crete after his death. The Agioi Deka (Holy Ten) (after whom the modern village is named) were martyred here during the rule of the emperor Decius (248-251), as was Bishop Cyril during the persecutions of Diocletian.

We have little evidence for the first Byzantine period in Crete. We know that there were bishoprics in the main cities (the texts put them as many as 22), and there are the ruins of large early Christian basilicas at Panormo, Vyzari, Knossos, Chersonessos, Gortys, Olous, Sitia, Falassarna, Kissamos, Elyros and elsewhere, that attest a peaceful way of life and a deeply held christian faith.

The sea protected Crete from the fearful invasions of the barbarians from the North. From the middle of the 7th century, however, the island began to be the object of attacks by the Arabs, who had developed a naval power based on N. Africa and Syria. The peace of the island was also disturbed in the 8th century by the iconoclast controversy. The Cretans sided from the very start with the iconodules, and supported the general Kosmas in his stance against Leo III.

The Arab Corquest (A.D. 824- 961)

In the 9th century, Saracen Arabs from Spain in search of a new country disembarked at the anchorage of Psari Foratha near Viannos. Abu Hafs Omar I, their leader, burned his boats in order to compel his soldiers to fight to the death to conquer this land flowing with milk and honey. The Cretans — especially the Cortynians — made a despairing struggle against him with the few means at their disposal, but in the end they were defeated by the fierce, antichristian foe. Cortyne was reduced to a pile of ruins. The Arab capital was built on the site of ancient Heraklion, and was surrounded with brick walls and deep moats. From the latter it took the name Khandax, which it retained, in its Venetian form "Candia" until the 19th century. The churches of Crete were either destroyed or converted into mosques, and the Cretans were compelled to change their faith. Crete once again became the head-quarters of fearsome pirates. In the bazaars of Khandax, eastern merchants bought the prisoners that came back in the pirate ships after their sudden attacks on islands and mainland alike. The Byzantines made many unsuccessful attempts to recapture the island, and it was only after 137 years, in A.D. 961, that the famous general, later emperor Nikiforos Fokas, with an enormous navy and army, succeeded in conquering and destroying the Arabs, after a siege lasting many moths, killing many and taking innumeral prisoners. Nothing remained standing in Khandax after its capture — even great part of the walls were razed to the ground.

The only relics of the Arab conquest of Crete that survive today are a series of Arab coins giving us the names of the Emirs of Crete.

Nikiforos Fokas made attempts to restore the hellenism and the religion of the island; he distributed Arab estates to many of his soldiers, and brought in new settlers from abroad. The mosques became churches once more and the Saints Nikon Metanoeite and John Xenos again proclaimed Christianity to the local population, who had been compelled to convert and forget the faith of their fathers. Nikiforos tried to move the city of Khandakas inland, to the fort of Temenos which he built on a peak near Youktas (modern Rokka, near Kanli Kastelli). This met with opposition on the part of the inhabitants however, and he was therefore compelled to rebuild the walls of Khandax; the city continued to be the capital, and the metropolis of the church of Crete was located there. The old bishoprics were revived, with the same names as before, but with their headquarters in different centres of their respective regions.

In the 12th century (A.D. 1182) new settlers were dispatched to Crete by the emperor Alexios II Komnenos, under the leadership of twelve young Byzantine aristocrats ('arkhontopouloi'), according to tradition, They were granted large tracts of land, and acquired great political authority, and their families formed a new Cretan aristocracy (Phokades, Kallergides, Gabalades, Mousouroi, Khortatzides, Melissinoi, Argyropouloi etc) They were soon to play a leading role in all the struggles against the Venetian conqueror.

The second Byzantine period in Crete has left a few small churches with interesting frescoes, the imposing ruins of the new church of St. Titus at Gortyna and the ruins of the Byzantine wals of Khandax. The art of Cretan portable icons, which produced a whole school, was born during this period. The icon of the Panagia kardiotissa, a 10th or 11th century work, still survives in Venice.

Venetian period (A.D. 1212-1669)

In 1204, when the Byzantine empire was broken up by the Crusaders and its territory divided amongst their leaders, Crete was granted to Boniface Momferatieus. He chose, however, to remain in Thessaloniki and to cede Crete to the Venetians in return for 1000 silver venetian marks and other, more important concessions. Before the Venetians could occupy the island, however, Genoan pirates under Erico Peskatori, Count of Malta, landed on it. They built forts on strategic sites, repaired the walls of Khandax, and successfully resisted the attacks of the Venetians until 1212, when the latter finally prevailed.

Under the new conqueror, Crete was divided for administrative purposes into 3, later 4, departments (diamerismata) that roughly corresponded with the modern nomoi, with the centre of authority in the main cities; there were also a larger number of kastellania centred around the strong Venetian castles, which in many cases were built on the same sites as the Genoan. Khandax, or Candia, was still the capital, and the whole island was named after it (REGNO DI CANDIA). It was here that the Duke settled with his council, as well as the Papal archbishop. The inhabitants were left to their orthodox faith, the lower ranking clergy were not persecuted, and the monasteries and their estates were left untouched; the church of Crete remained without a head, however, for the metropolitis and the orthodox bishops were compelled to leave the island.

A heavy tax was imposed on the population, great estates were granted to soldiers or colonists from Venice, and the Cretans were subjected to all kinds of oppression; all this provoked a long series of revolts, particularly during the first centuries of the Venetian occupation, which literally devastated Crete and gave rise to unimaginable acts of violence and savagery. There were revolts in 1212 itself, led by the Agiostefanites; in 1217, under the Melissinoi and Skordilles; in 1228 under the Arkoleoi, Melissinoi and Drakontopouloi, supported by Ioannis Vatatzis the king of Nikaia; in 1261, when Ioannis Palaiologos made an unsuccessful attempt to capture the island; and in 1271-77 under the leadership of the Chortatzides. Soon after this, Alexios Iergis succeeded in driving the conquerors out of the interior of the island and restricting them to the coast. This struggle was the largest of all; it went through many stages and ended in 1299 with the signing of a treaty between the two sides. The rebels were granted an amnesty, their estates, which had been confiscated, were restored to them, and they were given exemption from taxation for two years; Alexios Kallergis received a whole fief and other privileges, and ceased to fight against the Venetians. His family, however, continued to be in the forefront of subsequent revolts (1333, 1341, 1347 when, after an unsuccessful revolt the son of Alexios Leon was punished by being bound in a sack and thrown into the sea.)

Gradually, however, conquered and conquerors found a way of coming to an understanding in the strife-torn land. The strange power of the island to assimilate its inhabitants, and common interests and views brought local and foreign "Cretans" together in a unified revolt against the sovereign power of Venice. Crete was declared an independent "Republic of St. Titus" (1363), but was swiftly compelled to bow its head to the capital. In 1365, the Kallerges family renewed their struggles, causing further devastation of the country, for the Venetians burnt and destroyed forests, trees and crops in their attempts to capture the rebels.

Other, smaller uprisings followed in 1453 and 1462, and there was a major and final one in 1527 under the leadership of Kantanoleos or Lissoyiorgis.

The 15th and 16th centuries were marked by earth-quakes, piratical incursions, terrible famines and epidemics. Despite all its trials, however, Crete found the strength to heal its wounds, to create and to sing. The majority of its churches, with their frescoes, were built between the 13th and the 16th centuries' over 800 survive today, in varying states of preservation, in the villages, plains and mountains. Of particular interest are the **Panagia Keras** at Kritsa, **Agios Fanourios** at Valsamonero, **Panagia Kardiotissa** at Potamies and others.

After the capture of Constantinople by the Turks (1453), the Cretans locked the vision of the lost empire deep in their hearts, and drew closer to Venice, which took the place of the "City" in their thinking, and which they began to feel was somehow their own capital. As in ancient times, so now, Crete made its contribution to the new, wider European culture. Megalo Kastro (Heraklion) welcomed as refugees teachers of literature, theology and rhetoric and became a centre for the copying of Greek manuscripts which were brought from Constantinople and channeled to Italy by Byzantine scholars.

The Cretan Markos Mousouros, "the most cultured man of his age", published works by Sophocles, Euripides, Aristotle and Plato, on the press of Aldos Manoutios. At the same time Zakharias kallergis built the first purely Greek press and printed the great Etymological Lexicon of the Greek language, which made a very important contribution to Greek studies in Italy.

The western renaissance, in its turn, repaid the debt. Under its influence poetry sprang up in Cretan soil, in all its varied forms, and the theatre was reborn. Modern Greek literature has its roots in this flowering of Cretan letters, which produced works like the Erofili of Chortatzis, the Sacrifice of Abraham and the Erotokritos by Vicenzos kornaros. Cretan iconography took on new life, assimilating western elements, and Cretan portable icons were much sought after in the orthodox world. The most distinguished of the painters were Damaskinos, Theophanis of Crete and Emmanuel Tzanes Bounialis. The great Theotokopoulos (EL GRECO) served his apprenticeship in Cretan workshops during his early youth.

The architecture of the last centuries of Venetian rule, which was imitative of western models, left behind a rich inheritance in Crete, often stamping its character on a whole city or region: The defence works, produced by the toil and endeavours of Venetians and Cretans together, naturally occupy first place amongst the Venetian monuments. The new defence wall at Megalo Kastro enclosed both city and suburbs, (borghi) and was the biggest in the Eastern Mediterranean. It was built on the basis of plans drawn up by the famous architect SAMMICHELE. The imposing Fortetza at Rethymnon was intended to replace the entire city. The most powerful, the most impressive and the best preserved of the Venetian castles is the **Megalos Koules (CASTEL DEL MARE)** in Megalo Kastro; its stout walls have withstood the battering of the Cretan ocean for centuries.

Some of the great catholic churches that were built in the Cretan cities are still preserved, amongst them the basilica of St. Mark, and St. Peter in Heraklion, and St. Francisco in Chania and Rethymnon. The fine Venetian loggia of Candia in Palladian style has recently been rebuilt on the old plan; the "Armeria" is now the town hall of Heraklion; and the great dockyards in the harbour (arsenali) have been restored in their old form. The 'loggia' at Rethymnon houses the Archaeological Museum. The thirsty cities were beautified and refreshed by a large number of monumental fountains. The famous fountain of Morozini is still today one of the most impressive features of Heraklion, and the charming fountains of Priemuli and Benbo are also preserved there. The Duke's palace in Candia no longer survives, but one can see fine doorways from Venetian palaces in the Historical Museum of Crete and in the narrow streets of Chania and Rethymnon.

In the 16th and 17th centuries the orthodox monasteries also acquired large churches, built under the influence of western architecture (Arkadi, Moni Gonias, Moni Tsagarolon, Toplou etc.)

The final period of Venetian rule thus saw a reconciliation of the two opposed elements in Crete, in terms of art, literature, language, and even of creed. Soon they were to unite to face the common foe, the Turk, who was becoming an ever more menacing threat.

The Turkish period (1669 - 1898)

In 1645 the Turks succeeded in landing large forces to the west of Chania and gaining mastery over the island of Thodorou. They laid close siege to the city with an army of 25.000, and it was compelled to surrender, after resisting nobly. Rethymnon withstood the siege for two months, and within three years the whole island had passed into Turkish hands. 1648 saw the start of the legendary siege of Candia, the "Megalo Kastro", which resisted the enemy stubbornly for a period of 21 years, thus giving rise to one of the greatest epics in the modern history of Christianity.

Cretans and Venetians fought with courage and determination alongside each other, passing from hope to despair, from failure to success, working unceasingly at the defences and in the underground tunnels, playing a grim game of hide and seek in the passages that were being built continually by both sides, making heroic sallies, and keeping the harbour open for the relief forces sent from Venice and the West. This brief historical sketch does not permit of a true picture of the titanic struggle, which ended with the capitulation of the Christians in 1669. after a Venetian had treacherously betrayed all the weak points of the fortress to the Turks. The besieged were granted leave to depart in Venetian ships, taking with them whatever possessions and religious relics they could carry. Venice retained only her fortresses at Gramboussa, Souda and Spinalonga.

In Crete, the price paid for the unsuccessful struggle was high. Swingeing taxes were levied, public and private property was confiscated and distributed, in the form of muslim estates and buildings, to pashas, beys and agas, and murder, torture and compulsory conversion to Islam were common. Many Cretans became "Cryptochristians", while others sought refuge in the Venetian forts or the mountains. These resistance fighters in the mountains were a source of terror to the Turks, and were the first people to exact revenge on them.

It was naturally not long before organized resistance to the conqueror began, sometimes aided by Venice (1692) and sometimes encouraged by the Russians (revolt of Daskaloyanni in Sfakia in 1770): despite temporary successes, however, this resistance only led to greater oppression.

The fierce Turkish warriors (the jannissaries) held effective power on the island, and often found themselves at odds with the Turkish authorities themselves.

The Greek War of Independence in 1821 found Crete ready and determined to fight for her freedom. The struggle lasted for 10 years, with many twists of fortune, great successes and bitter defeats. It may be divided into two phases the first lasting until 1824, when large Egyptian forces called in by the Turks succeeded in putting down the rebels in a series of bloody battles. The second phase began in 1825 in Gramboussa, spread throughout the whole island and continued till 1830. At this point the Turks had been compelled to shut themselves up in their fortresses, but when the Protocol giving Greece its independence was signed in London, the island was omitted, and was driven by pressure from the Great Powers to submit. Once again Crete was "sold" by on lord to another, being ceded for 20.000.000 marks to Mehmet Ali of Egypt. The new occupation, which lasted until 1840, was no less oppressive, though the highhanded behaviour of the jannissaries was curbed. The taxes to finance public works- roads, bridges, acqueducts etc. imposed an intolerable burden on the exhausted Cretans, and a law providing for the compulsory cultivation of the land which effectively meant the confiscation of their farms, provoked a peaceful protest in the form of a great assembly demanding autonomy (Mournies, 1833); seventy of the most important participants in this assembly paid for it with their lifes.

In 1840 the island once more passed into the hands of the Turkish lord. The Cretans continued their struggle, however, now hoping for support form the Greek State and the Great Powers, and moving step by step towards their freedom, sometimes using force of arms and sometimes relying on diplomacy. There were uprisings in 1841, 1858, when they succeeded in improving temporarily the conditions of their servitude, and in 1866, with unofficial assistance from Greece in the form of units of volunteers under Greek officers, and large quantities of supplies. The great revolt lasted almost three years, and saw wonderful examples of heroism and self-sacrifice, culminating in the holocause of the besieged monastery at Arkadi. It eventually compelled Turkey, under pressure from the Great Powers to cede to the island the "Organikos Nomos" (Organic Statute).

Under its provisions Crete was named a General Administration, and its governor was advised by a muslim and a christian counsellor; the General Assembly was instituted, with equal representation from both sides and a wide jurisdiction; mixed courts were set up; and the unwritten right of the village elders to exercise judicial authority in disputes between Christians over inheritances, and family matters, was recognized.

The Turks, of course violated their agreements and promises on all kinds of pretexts. A new struggle in 1878 ended in the Convention of Chalepa, which granted to the Christians the right to self- administration that had been decided by the Powers at Berlin. This meant, amongst other things, a parliament with a Greek majority, the recognition of Greek as an official language, and the institution of a gendarmerie proportionately representing both sides. These privileges, however, were removed after a fresh, unsuccessful uprising at Kydonia which demanded union with Greece. In 1895 the Cretans once more revolted and successfully demanded the appointment of a Christian governor, the formation of a gendarmerie with European officers, and the economic and judicial independence of the island.

Finally, in 1897, Christians were slaughtered by a Turkish mob in Chania, and this provoked open, official intervention on the part of the Greek State, which sent an expeditionary force under the command of Colonel Timoleon Vassos in an attempt to occupy the island. Vassos made a successful descent at Kolymbari in W. Crete and achieved some initial victories, only to be informed by the Great Powers that they had occupied the cities, and that if he advanced towards Chania they would oppose him.

The Greek action led to the immediate outbreak of the unfortunate war between Greece and Turkey of 1897. The Cretans were compelled by events to accept autonomy under the Sultan proposed by the Powers, which they had so far rejected. While the "Executive", the temporary government of independent Crete was issuing its first orders, however, the Turkish mob again instigated a planned programme of slaughter and burning, this time in Heraklion. The English consuler and English soldiers are among the victims and the English consulat is burning. The military powers reaction effectively immediatly. The Turky are disarmed by the Navy detachments, hung the first who called for the trouble and make the Turky's coverment to retreat even the last soldier away from the Crete.

Cretan city. Union with Greece (1898-1912)

On December 9th, 1898, the first Lord, high Commisioner Crete, Prince George of Greece, set foot on Cretan soil to a deliriously emotional and enthusiastic welcome. The "Cretan State" was now a reality, and would soon have a constitution, an elected government, an internal administration, a bank, and issue its own coinage and stamps. The only reminder of Turkish sovereignty was the red star at one edge of the Greek Flag. The presence of the army of the Powers in the cities, however, and its fleet at Souda, still reminded the Cretans of their dream of a freedom without constraints and without need of protection. The demand for union with Greece appears repeatedly in the decisions of their assemblies, and even led to revolt (the movement of Venizelos at Therissos, 1905). Union was officially proclaimed by the Cretan people on several occasions, but each time the Powers prevented its implementation. When the war between Greece and Turkey broke out in 1912, El. Venizelos, the great politician from Chania, was prime minister of Greece. Steph. Dragoumis was despatched as general administrator of the island in the name of the Greek king, and Venizelos officially received representatives of the Cretan people in Parliament. Disguising his emotion the great Cretan, deeply conscious of the historical significance of the moment, announced laconically: "Gentlemen, I inform Parliament that from this moment Crete is an inseparable part of the Kingdom of Greece" (October 1st 1912).

These simple words, that gave to the troubled island its place in the Greek world, were the fruit of the fearful centuries-long cycle of torture, and of the bloody, determined ascent towards the light, which possesses all the qualities of a myth, or of a slow, heavy resistance song. The Cretan mind retains everything in its subconscious however, and the terrible memories have developed into an instinct for bravery and resistance that is now a typical Cretan characteristic, handed on from generation to generation.

The rizitika songs of the mountains and other folk-songs the mantinathes, the sound of the lyra and the proud dances were the main forms of Cretan artistic expression under Turkish rule. Art could not flourish in conditions of slavery, and during the continuous struggle for freedom. The creative activity of the Cretans was thus confined to simple, practical objects for daily use, and has a purely folk character. Cretan weaving in the 19th and the beginning of the 20th centuries produced creative compositions showing a wonderful use of colour and motif, wrought with great skill and patience. The wood-carvings too, worked in soft wood by men who were either resistance fighters or shepherds in the mountains, show that Crete never lost its natural artistic sensitivity.

The period of Turkish rule has left few notable architectural monuments on the island. The cities, of course assumed a Turkish character: cobbled streets, narrow lanes, houses with enclosed "chayati" latticed shutters and cool courtyards surrounded by high walls (often decorated with pebble mosaics), fountains with quotations from the Koran and flatly carved naturalising relief decoration, minarets, and Turkish graves with upright standing gravestones. New Turkish public buildings or mosques were very few, however, for the new conquerors used Venetian buildings for their own purposes (walls, forts, barracks, churches, etc), after converting them more or less extensively.

The Turkish element lived in peace with the Christian from the time of union with Greece until 1923, when they were compelled to leave the island by the major exchange of populations.

The German occupation (1941 - 44).

When the Germans launched their air offensive in order to capture Crete, in May 1941, the island had been stripped of all its soldiers, who had been sent to fight in Albania, and no real preparation had been made for its defence. The memories stirred in the blood, however, and the Cretan instinct awoke all-powerful in men, women and children alike. The strange battle between fully-armed paratroops on one side and the Cretans fighting with primitive weapons on the other lasted for 10 whole days, and destroyed the picked German force, thus delaying the German attack on Russia. The cycle of hell was renewed however. Life in the ruined cities became difficult and dark, the jails were filled with martyrs the mountains came to life again with indomitable resistance fighters, streams echoed to the bullets from machine guns riddling the unprotected bodies of hostages, death loomed in the air, and forgotten prophecies found their way into men's hearts to keep hope alive.

The bloody cycle was short-lived this time and ended in October 1944, when the occupation army was withdrawn to a bridge head in the Souda-Akrotiri area, to wait to surrender to the allies. Crete again buried its memories and set to work to heal its wounds. Not many years passed before the former occupiers became friends. Many of them had lived on the blood-stained island during its most difficult hours, and did not forget that for all its tribulations it still knew how to smile- even at the enemy, whom it often felt was trapped in the same nightmare. They came back with their wives, children and friends along with thousands of visitors from all over the world, to see once more the wild, proud mountains, the sparkling, foaming coasts, the peaceful valleys, the deep gorges, the magical ancient cities the unique works of art in the Museums, and the direct, wakeful gaze of the men, and to taste again the fruits of the soil and the sweet Cretan wine.

It is not too extravagant to claim that anyone who has lived in Crete, friend or foe feels a nostalgia within him, as though for a lost fatherland, and that whoever once visits the island returns. And the island is ever more equipped not to disappoint its visitors, and to ensure them a happy and pleasant stay.

HISTORY OF THE EXCAVATIONS
AT KNOSSOS

It had long been known that there had once existed a city called Knossos in this region, and indeed, the inhabitants often found ancient objects as they cultivated their fields.

The first man to excavate in the area was Minos Kalokairinos, a merchant of Heraklion, and a lover of antiquity. In 1878 he uncovered two of the palace store-rooms. The Turkish owners of the land compelled him to stop his investigations, and the attempts of Schliemann to purchase the "Kefala" hill came to nought because of the excessive sums they demanded. Fortune thus played a part in assisting Arthur Evans to begin systematic excavation in 1900, when the island had now been declared an independent State. He was at that time Director of the Ashmolean Museum in Oxford, and first visited Crete in order to study and decipher the unknown script that could be made out on sealstones.

The excavations began at a very rapid pace, and by the end of 1903 almost all of the palace had been uncovered and work began on the surrounding area. Evans continued his researches until 1931, with an interruption for the duration of the First World War. He subsequently published his work in four volumes entitled "The Palace of Minos at Knossos". His chief assistant was the archaeologist D. Mackenzie, who kept the basic day-book of the excavations.

From the beginning it proved necessary to preserve and restore the monuments that were being uncovered. A number of parts of the palace were restored in this way, and considerable use was made of reinforced cement in the work. The parts of the restoration that represent timber frames and other wooden structures were formerly painted yellow (the yellow colour has now been replaced by a colour conventionally representing the wood). In a number of places, moreover, copies were installed of the marvellous frescoes discovered during the excavation of the palace. This method of restoration has received much criticism, since it used materials foreign to Minoan architecture. Some scholars also dispute some of the conclusions of the pioneer English excavator.

All these questions aside, E v a n s is, constantly admired for his intuition, his creative imagination and his profound scholarship. It is basically to him that we owe the discovery of the marvellous Minoan world, which until his time was only dimly reflected in Greek Mythology. His services have brought him international fame and recognition.

As a mark of honour, therefore, and to perpetuate his memory, his bust has been erected on the south side of the west court of the palace.

After his death responsibility for the excavations at Knossos, which continue to the present day, was assumed by the British School of Archaeology.

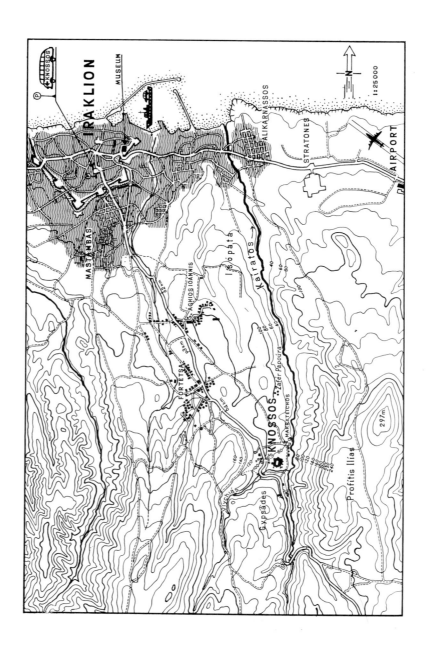

CR

Iouis magni, me

omnibus geogra

AEGAEVM

Creticum mare

CYDONES

ETEO CRE

Africum siue Lybicum mare

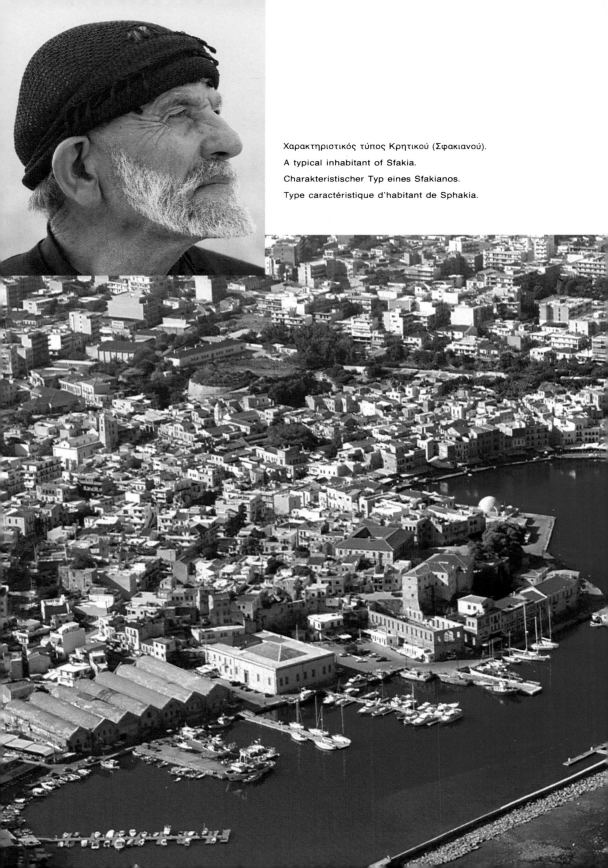

Χαρακτηριστικός τύπος Κρητικού (Σφακιανού).

A typical inhabitant of Sfakia.

Charakteristischer Typ eines Sfakianos.

Type caractéristique d'habitant de Sphakia.

XANIA - CHANIA

Η πόλη Χανιά, πρωτεύουσα του ομώνυμου Νομού στο δυτικότερο τμήμα του νησιού. Είναι χτισμένη πάνω στην αρχαία Κυδωνία. Αποικίστηκε από τους Βενετσιάνους το 1252. Έχει πληθυσμό 60.000 κατοίκους.

The city of Chania, administrative capital of the *Nomos* of the same name in the West of the island. Built over ancient Kydonia, it was colonised by the Venetians in 1252. It has a population of about 60.000.

Die Stadt Chania, Hauptstadt des gleichnamigen Bezirkes im westlichsten Teil der Insel. Sie ist auf dem alten Kydonia errichtet. Sie wurde 1252 von den Venezianern kolonisiert. Sie hat eine Bevölkerung von ca 60.000 Einwohnern.

La ville de la Canée, chef-lieu du département du même nom, dans la partie occidentale de l' île. Elle est construite sur l'ancienne ville Kydonia. Elle a été colonisée par les Vénitiens en 1252. Elle compte environ 60.000 habitants.

Το Βενετσιάνικο λιμάνι των Χανίων και ο Φάρος. Από τα πιο όμορφα μεσαιωνικά λιμάνια της Ευρώπης. Ιδανικό για τον ελλιμενισμό μικρών σκαφών.

The Venetian Harbour of Chania, with the lighthouse. It is one of the most beautiful medieval harbours in Europe, and is ideal for mooring small boats.

Der venezianische Hafen von Chania und der Leuchtturm. Einer der schönsten mittelalterlichen Häfen Europas. Ideal als Anlegeplatz kleiner Schiffe.

Le port Vénitien de la Canée avec son phare. C'est un des plus beaux ports moyenâgeux d'Europe, et il est idéal pour l'ancrage de bateaux de petit tonnage.

Βενετσιάνικα στενά στην παλιά πόλη των Χανίων.

Narrow Venetian streets in the old city of Chania.

Venezianische Enggassen in der Altstadt von Chania.

Ruelles vénitiennes dans la vieille ville de la Canée.

Η δημοτική αγορά Χανίων. Έχει σχήμα σταυρού, με πόρτες σε κάθε πλευρά, και 80 καταστήματα με όλα τα είδη τροφίμων.

The (public) market at Chania. It is shaped like a cross with porches in each side, and has 80 shops selling every kind of foodstuff.

Die Markthalle von Chania. Sie ist kreuzförmig angelegt, mit Türen an jedem Endpunkt des Kreuzes und 80 Geschäften mit allen Lebensmittelartikeln.

Le marché municipal de la Canée. En forme de croix, avec des portes sur les quatre côtés, il abrite 80 magasins de produits alimentaires.

Ελευθέριος Βενιζέλος (1864-1936). Από τους μεγαλύτερους πολιτικούς της νεώτερης Ελλάδος.

Eleutherios Venizelos (1864-1936). One of the greatest politicians of Greece in modern times.

Eleutherios Venizelos (1864-1936). Einer der größten Politiker des neuzeitlichen Griechenlands.

Eleuthère Vénizelos (1864-1936). Un des plus grands hommes politiques de la Grèce moderne.

Το γερμανικό νεκροταφείο στο Μάλεμε, σε ύψωμα 107 μ.

The German cemetery at Maleme, on a hill 107 m. high.

Der deutsche Friedhof in Maleme, auf einer Höhe von 107m.

Le cimetière allemand à Malémè, sur une butte de 107 m.

Το λιμάνι της Σούδας, που εξυπηρετεί σήμερα την ατμοπλοϊκή συγκοινωνία των Χανίων. Ο κόλπος της Σούδας, από τους μεγαλύτερους και ασφαλέστερους της Μεσογείου, είναι το σταυροδρόμι της ναυτιλιακής κίνησης στη Μεσόγειο.

The harbour of Souda, which is nowadays the terminal for steamships to Chania. Souda bay is one of the largest and safest in the Mediterranean, and is a crossroad for Mediterranean shipping.

Der Hafen von Suda, der heute dem Dampferkhehr von Chania dient. Die Bucht von Suda, eine der größten und sichersten des Mittelmeeres, ist der Kreuzweg der Schiffahrt im Mittelmeer.

Le port de Souda qui dessert aujourd'hui les communications maritimes de la Canée. La baie de Souda, une des plus grandes et des plus abritées de la Méditerranée, constitue un des carrefours des transports maritimes de la Méditerranée.

Το αγγλικό νεκροταφείο στο μυχό του κόλπου της Σούδας.

The English cemetery in the heart of Souda Bay.

Der englische Friedhof im innersten Winkel der Suda-Bucht.

Le cimetière anglais au fond de la baie de Souda.

Το οροπέδιο Ασκύφου με το ομώνυμο γραφικό χωριό.

The plateau of Askyphou, and the pretty village of the same name.

Die Hochebene Askyphou mit dem gleichnamigen malerischen Dorf.

Le plateau d' Askyphou avec le joli village du même nom.

Χώρα Σφακίων. Παράλιο γραφικό χωριό στο Λιβυκό Πέλαγος.

Chora Sfakion, a picturesque seaside village on the Libyan sea.

Chora Sfakion. Malerisches Küstendorf am Libyschen Meer.

Chora de Sphakia. Beau village au bord de la Mer Libyque.

Το Φραγκοκάστελλο, στη Νότια ακτή της Κρήτης.

The «Frangokastello» on the South coast of Crete.

Das Frankokastello an der Südküste Kretas.

La «Franco Castello» sur la côte sud de la Crète.

Η παραλία της Παλαιοχώρας στη Νότια
ακτή της Κρήτης.

The beautiful beach of Palaiochora
on the South coast of Crete.

Der Strand von Paleochora an der
Südküste Kretas.

La merveilleuse baie de Paléochora
sur la côte Sud de la Crète.

Η Μονή Χρυσοσκαλίτισσας, στη δυτική άκρη της
Κρήτης. Η παράδοση έλεγε πως ένα από τα 90
σκαλοπάτια που οδηγούν στη κορυφή του βράχου
ήταν ολόχρυσο και πως από αυτό πήρε το όνομα
Χρυσοσκαλίτισσα.

Moni Chryssoskalitissa, on the west coast of Crete.
According to the tradition, one of the 90 steps
leading to the pinnacle of the rock was made of
gold, and this is how the nunnery got its name
(Chryssoskalitissa – 'of the golden step').

Das Kloster Chryssoskalitissa (Goldtreppchen), am
westlichen Ende Kretas. Die Überlieferung sagte,
daß eine der 90 Stufen, die auf die Felsspitze
führen, aus purem Gold war und daß es von daher
den Namen Chryssoskalitissa bekam.

Le monastère de Chryssoskalitissa, sur la côte
occidentale de l'île. La tradition dit que l'une des
90 marches qui conduisent au sommet du rocher
était en or, et que c'est pourquoi le monastère a
pris le nom de Chryssoskalitissa, qui veut dire
Vierge de l' escalier d'or'.

Λίμνη Κουρνά. Είναι η μοναδική λίμνη της Κρήτης. Έχει περιφέρεια 3,5 χλμ. έκταση 1,4 τετ. χλμ. και βάθος 45 μ. Μέσα στη λίμνη υπάρχουν δυο πλούσιες πηγές. Το αρχαίο όνομα της λίμνης ήταν «Κορησία».

The Lake of Kourna, the only lake on Crete. It has a circumference of 3,5 kms, an area of 1,4 square kms, and is 45 metres deep. There are two rich springs within the lake, the ancient name of which was 'Korissia'.

Der See Kourna. Es ist der einzige See Kretas. Er hat einen Umfang von 3,5 km, eine Fläche von 1,4 qkm und eine Tiefe von 45 m. In dem See gibt es zwei reichhaltige Quellen. Der alte Name des Sees war 'Korissia'.

Le lac Kourna. C'est le seul lac de Crète. Il a 3,5 km de circonférence, 1,4 km^2 et 45 m de profondeur. Il est alimenté par deux sources abondantes qui se trouvent au fond. Son nom antique est 'Korissia'.

Μονή Γουβερνέτου ή της «Κυρίας των Αγγέλων». Βρίσκεται στη ΒΑ άκρη του ακρωτηρίου Μελέχας και χτίστηκε στη σημερινή μορφή της τον 17ο αιώνα. Ιδρύθηκε από τους μοναχούς του βυζαντινού μοναστηριού Αγ. Ιωάννου του Ερημίτη, που σώζεται σε γειτονικό φαράγγι.

Moni Gouvernetou, or Tis Kyrias ton Angelon, on the N.E. end of the Melechas promontory. It was built in its present form in the 17th century. It was founded by the monks of the Byzantine monastery of Ay. Ioannis the Erimitis, which survives in the gorge nearby.

Kloster Gouverneto oder der Muttergottes. Es befindet sich auf der nordöstlichen Spitze des Kaps Melechas, und wurde im 17. Jahrhundert in seiner heutigen Form erbaut. Es wurde von den Mönchen des byzantinischen Kloster Ag. Joannis, des Eremiten, gegründet, das noch in der benachbarten Schlucht erhalten ist.

Le monastère de Gouverneto ou de la Vierge des Anges. Il se trouve au Nord-Est du cap Mélekhas, et a été construit sous sa forme actuelle au XVIIème s., par des moines du monastère byzantin de St. Jean l' Erimite, qui existe encore, dans une gorge voisine.

Το περίφημο φαράγγι της Σαμαριάς, στο οροπέδιο του Ομαλού. Έχει μήκος 18 χλμ., πλάτος 2-40 μέτρα και βάθος από 250-600 μέτρα. Στις λεγόμενες «πόρτες» στενεύει σε 2-3 μέτρα. Το τέρμα του φαραγγιού βρίσκεται στην Αγία Ρουμέλη, στην παραλία του Λιβυκού Πελάγους.

The famous gorge of Samaria, on the plateau of Omalos. It is 18 kms. long, from 2 to 40 metres wide, and from 250-600 metres deep. At the so-called 'doors' it narrows to 2-3 metres. The gorge ends at Ayia Roumeli on the Libyan Ocean.

Die berühmte Samaria-Schlucht, in der Hochebene von Omalos. Sie hat eine Länge von 18 km, eine Breite von 2-40 m und ihre Tiefe liegt zwischen 250-600 m. Bei den sogenannten 'Portes' (Toren) verengt sie sich auf 2-3 m. Die Schlucht endet in Agia Roumeli, an der Küste des Libyschen Meeres.

La fameuse gorge de Samaria, sur le plateau d' Omalos. Elle a 18 km., de long, de 2 à 40 m de large, et de 250 à 600 m de profondeur. A certains endroits, que l'on appelle les 'portes', elle se resserre jusqu'à 2 ou 3 m. La gorge parvient à Haghia Roumeli, sur le côté de la mer de Libye.

Η ωραία παραλία του Ρεθύμνου που
απλώνεται σε μάκρος 12 χλμ.

The fine beach at Rethymno, which
stretches for 12 kms.

Der schöne Strand von Rethymno, der sich
über 12 km erstreckt.

La magnifique plage de Réthymno, qui
s'étend sur 12 km.

ΡΕΘΥΜΝΟ - RETHYMNO

Η πόλη Ρέθυμνο, στο κέντρο της βόρειας παραλίας του νησιού, είναι πρωτεύουσα του ομώνυμου νομού. Στη θέση του σημερινού Ρεθύμνου υπήρχε η αρχαία Ρίθυμνα. Έχει πληθυσμό περίπου 18.000 κατοίκους.

The city of Rethymno, in the middle of the north coast of the island, is the administrative capital of the *nomos* of the same name. Ancient Rithymna stood on the site of the modern city. It has about 18.000 inhabitants.

Die Stadt Rethymno, im Zentrum der Nordküste der Insel, ist die Hauptstadt des gleichnamigen Bezirkes und hat eine Bevölkerung von ungefähr 18.000 Einwohnern.

La ville de Réthymno est située au milieu de la côté Nord de l' île. C'est le chef-lieu du département du même nom. À cet emplacement se dressait l' antique Rithymna. Elle compte environ 18.000 habitants.

Η εκκλησία της Μονής Αρκαδίου. Η πιο διάσημη ιστορική μονή της Κρήτης, το ιερότερο σύμβολο της κρητικής λευτεριάς. Στην επανά-σταση του 1866 ενάντια στους Τούρκους η μονή ανατινάχθηκε στις 9 του Νοέμβρη από τον Κωστή Γιαμπουδάκη, θάβοντας κάτω από τα ερείπιά της μαζί με τους πολιορκούμενους Κρητικούς (864 άνδρες και γυναικόπαιδα) διπλάσιους πολιορκητές.

Moni Arkadiou, the most famous monastery in Crete and the most sacred symbol of Cretan freedom. During the revolt of 1866 against the Turks, the monastery was blown up by Kostis Yambouthakis, on November 9. The besieged Cretans (864 men, women and children) were buried in the ruins, along with double that number of the besiegers.

Das Kloster Arkadi. Das berühmteste historische Kloster Kretas, das heiligste Symbol der kretischen Freiheit. Beim Aufstand von 1866 gegen die Türken wurde das Kloster am 9. November von Kostis Jamboudakis in die Luft gesprengt, wobei er zusammen mit den belagerten Kretern (864 Männern, Frauen und Kindern) und mit doppelt sovielen Belagerern unter den Trümmern des Klosters begraben wurde.

Le monastère d' Arkadi. De point de vu historique, c' est le plus célèbre monastère de Crète, et le plus sacré des symboles de l'indépendance crétoise. Lors de la révolution de 1866 contre les Turcs, Kostis Giamboudhakis le fit sauter le 9 Novembre 864 Crétois, hommes, femmes et enfants qui y avaient cherché refuge, furent ensevelis sous ses décombres, avec un nombre double d' assié-geants.

Αγία Γαλήνη. Παράλιο γραφικό χωριό στον κόλπο της Μεσαράς.

Ayia Galini, a pretty coast village in the bay of Messara.

Agia Galini. Malerisches Küstendorf in der Bucht von Messara.

Haghia Galini, joli village dans le golfe de la Messara.

Η Πλατεία Ελευθερίας. (Τρεις καμάρες).

Plateia Eleutherias (Three Arches).

Der Freiheitsplatz (Tris Kamares).

La place Eleutherias.

Ο Τάφος του Νίκου Καζαντζάκη, στον Προμαχώνα Μαρτινέγκο.

The Grave of Nikos Kazantzakis.

Das Grab von Nikos Kazantzakis auf der Bastion Martinengo.

Le Tombeau de Nicos Kazantzakis sur le bastion Martinengo.

Το φρούριο Κούλες, ένα από τα επιβλητικότερα βενετσιάνικα μνημεία της Κρήτης, με μερική άποψη της πόλης.

The fort in the harbour (Koules), one of the most imposing Venetian monuments in Crete, and a view of part of Heraklion.

Die Festung Koules, eines der gebieterischsten Venezianischen Monumente Kretas und Teilansicht der Stadt.

Le fort du port d' Héraclion (Koulès), un des plus impressionnants monuments vénitiens de Crète, avec une vue partielle sur la ville.

Κρήνη Μοροζίνι. Θαυμάσιο έργο του προβλεπτή Φραγκ. Μοροζίνι. Από τα στόματα των λιονταριών έτρεχε νερό, για να δείξει ότι το Ηράκλειο απόκτησε άφθονο νερό.

The fountain of Morozini. Built in the 17th century by the Venetian Proveditor Franc. Morozini, along with a new acqueduct.

Morosini-Brunnen. Wundervolles Werk errichtet von Franz. Morosini. Aus den Mäulern der Löwen floß Wasser, um zu zeigen, daß Heraklion reich an Wasser war.

La fontaine de Morosini. Elle a été construite au XVIIè s. par le provéditaire Frang. Morosini, à l'occasion de la création d'un nouvel aqueduc.

Η «Λότζια». Από τα λαμπρότερα μνημεία της Βενετοκρατίας στην Κρήτη. Ήταν λέσχη για τις συγκεντρώσεις και την αναψυχή των ευγενών.

The "Loggia". One of the finest Venetian monuments in Crete. It was a club at which the nobles could gather and relax.

Die "Loggia". Eines der leuchtendsten Denkmäler der venezianischen Herrschaft auf Kreta. Es war der Klub für die Zusammenkünfte und die Erholung der Adligen.

La "Loggia", un des plus beaux monuments vénitiens de Crète. C'était un cercle, lieu de rencontre et de détente pour l'aristocratie.

ΗΡΑΚΛΕΙΟ - HERAKLIO

Η πόλη Ηράκλειο στο κέντρο της βόρειας παραλίας του νησιού, είναι πρωτεύουσα του ομώνυμου νομού και η μεγαλύτερη από τις άλλες πόλεις της Κρήτης, με πληθυσμό περίπου 110.000 κατοίκους. Χτίστηκε από τους Άραβες το 824 μ.Χ. και λεγόταν Χάνδαξ. Στην αρχαία εποχή ήταν το επίνειο της Κνωσού. Περιβάλλεται από παλιά ενετικά τείχη. Η σύγχρονη πόλη έχει επεκταθεί έξω από τα τείχη. Η πόλη και όλη η περιφέρεια του νομού έχει να δείξει πολλά: αρχαιολογικά και ιστορικά μνημεία, Μουσεία, βιβλιοθήκες, ωδείο, ξενοδοχεία, διεθνές αεροδρόμιο κ.λπ. Από το λιμάνι του Ηρακλείου γίνεται μεγάλο εξαγωγικό εμπόριο.

The city is the administrative capital of the *nomos* of the same name, and is the largest in Crete, with a population of 110.000. It lies in the middle of the north coast of the island. Founded in A.D. 824 by the Arabs, it was named Khandak after the defence ditches; it was called Khandax in the Byzantine period, and Candia in the Venetian. In ancient times Heraklion was the port for Knossos. The City, and indeed the whole *nomos,* has much *to* offer: archaeological and historical sites and monuments, museums, libraries, hotels, facilities for tourists, an international airport and so on. There is a great export-trade through the port of Heraklion.

Die Stadt Heraklion im Zentrum der Nordküste der Insel ist Hauptstadt des gleichnamigen Bezirkes und die größte von allen Städten Kretas. Sie hat eine Bevölkerung von ungefähr 110.000 Einwohnern. Sie wurde im Jahre 824 n. Chr. von den Arabern erbaut und hieß Chandax, von den Byzantinern und Candia von den Venezianern. In der antiken Epoche war sie der Ankerplatz von Knossos. Die Stadt und die ganze Umgebung des Bezirkes haben viel zu zeigen: archäologische und historische Monumente, Museen, Bibliotheken, Konservatorium, Hotels, internationalen Flughafen usw. Vom Hafen Heraklions aus wird ein großer Exporthandel betrieben.

Héraclion est le chef-lieu du département et, avec ses 110.000 habitants, la plus grande ville de Crète. Elle est située au milieu de la côte Nord de l'île. Fondée par les Arabes en 824, elle a été appelée Handak, du mot qui signifie la fossé des fortifications; à l'époque byzantine, on l'appelait Khandax, et sous les Vénitiens Candia. Dans l'antiquité, Héraclion était le port de Cnossos. La ville même et tout le département sont pleins de ressources: sites archéologiques et historiques, monuments, musées, bibliothèques, hôtels, installations touristiques, aéroport international. Le port d' Héraclion est un grand centre d' exportation.

Το κουλούρι του γάμου.
The wedding bread (koulouri).
Das Hochzeitsbrot.
Le pain de mariage.

Θαυμάσιο κρητικό χειροποίητο κέντημα.
A marvellous hand-made Cretan embroidery.
Wundervolle kretische handgefertigte Stickerei.
Magnifique broderie crétoise.

Γάμος. Στα Ανώγεια, την ωραία και ηρωική κωμόπολη με τα γνήσια κρητικά έθιμα, ένας γάμος εξακολουθεί να αποτελεί για όλους τους κατοίκους αφορμή χαράς και γλεντιού.

A wedding. In the fine, heroic village of Anoyia the true Cretan customs are preserved, and a wedding is still an occasion for all the inhabitants to rejoice and celebrate.

Hochzeit. In Anoja, dem schönen und heldenhaften Dorf mit den echten kretischen Gebräuchen ist eine Hochzeit heute noch für alle Einwohner ein Anlaß zur Freude und zur Feier.

Mariage. A Anoyia, belle bourgade au passé glorieux, la tradition reste vivace, et un mariage constitue encore aujourd'hui un jour de joie et de fête pour tous les habitants.

Υφάντρα στον αργαλειό. Τα πολύχρωμα μαλλιά επιτρέπουν στην υφάντρα να φτιάχνει πολυποίκιλα σχέδια. Είναι μια τέχνη που περνά ακόμα και σήμερα από μάνα σε κόρη.

Woman (weaving) at the loom. The multicoloured wool makes it possible for her to weave complicated designs. The art is still today handed on from mother to daughter.

Weberin am Webstuhl. Die vielfarbige Wolle erlaubt der Weberin eine reiche Auswahl an Mustern herzustellen. Es ist eine Kunst, die auch heute noch von Mutter zu Tochter weitergegeben wird.

Tisseuse à son métier. Les laines multicolores permettent l'exécution de dessins extrêmement variés. C'est un art qui aujourd'hui hui encore passe de mère en fille.

Η «Θεία Λειτουργία». Μια από τις έξι εικόνες του Μιχαήλ Δαμασκηνού (16ος αι.) που βρίσκονται στην Αγία Αικατερίνη Ηρακλείου.

"Missa Solemnis". One of the six icons by Michael Damaskinos (16th cent.) kept in the church of S. Catherine, Heraklion.

Die "Missa Solemnis". Eine der sechs Ikonen des Malers Michael Damaskinos (16 Jahrhundert), die in der Kirche von S. Katherina in Heraklion aufbewahrt sind.

La "Messe Solennelle". Une de six icones de Michel Damaskinos (16ème s.), qui sont conservées à l' église de S. Cathérine, Héraclion.

ΤΟ ΑΡΧΑΙΟΛΟΓΙΚΟ ΜΟΥΣΕΙΟ ΗΡΑΚΛΕΙΟΥ
ARCHAEOLOGICAL MUSEUM

Το Αρχαιολογικό Μουσείο ιδρύθηκε από τον «Φιλεκπαιδευτικό Σύλλογο» στα τέλη του περασμένου αιώνα. Πρώτοι διευθυντές του ήταν οι λαμπροί επιστήμονες Ιωσήφ Χατζιδάκης και Στέφανος Ξανθουδίδης. Το κτίριο που τελείωσε στις παραμονές του Β΄ Παγκοσμίου πολέμου, στεγάζει πολύτιμες συλλογές όλων των εποχών του αρχαίου κρητικού πολιτισμού. Στις αίθουσές του έχουν εκτεθεί με χρονολογική σειρά ευρήματα νεολιθικών, μινωικών (προανακτορικών, παλαιοανακτορικών, νεοανακτορικών, μετανακτορικών) και ελληνικών (γεωμετρικών, αρχαϊκών, κλασικών και ελληνορωμαϊκών) χρόνων. Ιδιαίτερες αίθουσες έχουν διατεθεί για τις σαρκοφάγους, τις τοιχογραφίες, την πρώην συλλογή Γιαμαλάκη κ.ά.

The Archaeological Museum was founded by the "Philekpaideutikos Syllogos" at the end of the last century. The first directors were the distinguished scholars Joseph Chatzidakis and Stephanos Xanthoudidis. The building, which was completed on the eve of the Second World War, houses valuable collections representing all the periods of ancient Cretan civilisation. The rooms contain exhibits in chronological order; of neolithic period, Minoan (pre-palace; first palace; second palace; post palace), and Greek (geometric, archaic, classical, Greco-Roman). There are separate rooms for the sarcophagi, the frescoes, the former Yamalakis collection, and so on.

Das Archäologische Museum wurde von dem "Verein der Bildungsfreunde" zu Ende des vorigen Jahrhunderts gestiftet. Seine ersten Direktoren waren die ausgezeichneten Wissenschaftler Joseph Chatzidakis und Stephan Xanthoudidis. Sein Gebäude, das in den Vortagen des 2. Weltkrieges fertiggestellt wurde, beherbergt wertvolle Sammlungen aller Epochen der antiken kretischen Kultur. In seinen Sälen sind in chronologischer Reihenfolge die Funde der neolithischen, minoischen, (Vorpalast, älteren Palast-, jüngeren Palast und der Nachpalstzeit), der griechischen (geometrischen, archaischen, klassischen und griechisch-römischen) Jahre aufgestellt. Gesonderte Säle sind den Sarkophagen, den Fresken, der früheren Sammlung Jamalakis u.a. vorbehalten.

Le Musée Archéologique d' Héraclion a été fondé par l'Association des amis de l'Éducation à la fin du siècle dernier. Ses premiers directeurs ont été les grands savants Joseph Chadzidakis et Stéphanos Xanthoudidis. Le bâtiment actuel, terminé à la veille de la deuxième guerre mondiale, abrite de précieuses collections d' objets de toutes les époques de la civilisation crétoise antique. Dans les salles, sont exposés en ordre chronologique des trouvailles des époques néolithique, minoenne (prépalatiale, protopalatiale, néopalatiale et postpalatiale), grecque (géométrique, archaïque, classique, hellénistique et greco-romaine). Des salles spéciales sont consacrées aux sarcophages, aux fresques, à l' ancienne collection Giamalakis, etc.

Θαυμάσιο ρυτό από στεατίτη σε σχήμα κεφαλής ταύρου. Τα κέρατα ήταν επίχρυσα, τα μάτια από ορεία κρύσταλλο και το ρύγχος από σεντέφι. Μικρό ανάκτορο Κνωσού, 16ος αιώνας π.Χ.

Wonderful steatite rhyton in the shape of a bull's head. The horns were gilded, the eyes made of rock crystal and the muzzle of mother-of-pearl. Little palace at Knossos. 16th century B.C.

Wundervolles Ryton (Trankopfervase) aus Steatit in Form eines Stierkopfes. Die Hörner waren vergoldet, die Augen aus Bergkristall und das Maul aus Perlmutter. Kleiner Palast von Knossos, 16. Jh. v. Chr.

Magnifique rhython de stéatite, en forme de tête de taureau. Les cornes étaient dorées, les yeux faits de cristal de roche et les naseaux de nacre. Petit palais de Cnossos, 16ème s. av. J.-C.

Η περίφημη «Παριζιάνα», ιέρεια της θεότητας. Από τοιχογραφία της Κνωσού, 15ος αιώνας π.Χ.

The famous "Parisienne", a priestess of the deity. From a fresco at Knossos, 15th century B.C.

Die berühmte "Pariserin", Priesterin der Gottheit. Von einem Fresko aus Knossos, 15. Jh. v. Chr.

La célèbre "Parisienne", prêtresse de la divinité. Fragment d' une fresque de Cnossos, 15ème s. av. J.-C.

Η μεγαλύτερη «Θεά των όφεων», ειδώλιο από φαγεντιανή. Στα απλωμένα χέρια της Θεάς τυλίγεται το φίδι, που φτάνει ως επάνω, στο ψηλό κάλυμμα του κεφαλιού της. Η θεά φορεί μακρύ φόρεμα με ποδιά και έχει το στήθος της γυμνό. Βρέθηκε στο Θησαυροφυλάκιο του κεντρικού ιερού του ανακτόρου της Κνωσού και χρονολογείται γύρω στα 1600 π.Χ.

The larger "Snake Goddess", a faience figurine. The snake is winding round the outstretched arms of the goddess and is stretching towards the high tiara on her head. The goddess is wearing a long dress with an apron, and her breasts are bare. Found in the treasuries of the central shrine of the palace at Knossos. About 1600 B.C.

Die größere "Schlangengöttin", Idol aus Fayence. Die Schlange windet sich um die ausgebreiteten Arme der Göttin und reicht bis oben an ihre hohe Kopfbedeckung. Die Göttin trägt ein langes Kleid mit Schürze und ihre Brust ist entblößt. Sie wurde gefunden in den Schazkammern des Zentralheiligtums des Palastes von Knossos und datiert um 1600 v. Chr.

La plus grande des "déesses aux serpents". Figurine de faience. Un serpent s'enroule autour de ses bras étendus et se dresse audessus de sa haute coiffure. La déesse porte une jupe longue avec un tablier, et a la poitrine nue. Elle a été trouvée dans les trésors sacrés du sanctuaire central du palais de Cnossos et date des environs de 1600 av. J. -C.

Η μικρότερη «Θεά των όφεων», άλλο ειδώλιο από φαγεντιανή που βρέθηκε στις κρύπτες του κεντρικού ιερού του ανακτόρου της Κνωσού. Γύρω στα 1600 π.Χ.

The smallest «Snake Goddess», a faience figurine discovered in the crypts of the central shrine of the palace at Knossos about 1600 B.C.

Die kleinere «Schlangengöttin», ein anderes Idol aus Fayence, das in den Krypten des Zentralheiligtums des Palastes von Knossos gefunden wurde. Um 1600 v. Chr.

La plus petite «déesse aux serpents», autre statuette de faience, trouvée dans les cryptes du sanctuaire central du palais de Cnossos. Alentours de 1600 av. J.-C.

Χρωματιστό ανάγλυφο του «Πρίγκηπα με τα κρίνα» ή «Βασιλιά - Αρχιερέα». Φορεί το μινωικό περίζωμα και έχει στο κεφάλι περίτεχνο στέμμα από κρίνα και φτερά παγωνιού. Με το αριστερό του χέρι τραβούσε ίσως κάποιο ιερό ζώο. Ανάκτορο Κνωσού, τέλος του 15ου αιώνα π.Χ.

Coloured relief of the ''Prince with the Lilies'' or ''Priest-King''. He is wearing the Minoan cod-piece and has a superb crown of lilies and peacock's feathers on his head. He may have been leading some sacred animal with his left hand. Palace of Knossos; end of the 15th century B.C.

Farbiges Relief des ''Prinzen mit den Lilien'' oder ''Priesterkönigs''. Er trägt den minoischen Lenden-schurz und hat auf dem Kopf eine kunstvolle Krone aus Lilien und Pfauenfedern. Mit der linken Hand zog er vermutlich irgendeines heiliges Tier. Palast von Knossos, Ende des 15. Jh. v. Chr.

Fresque en relief du ''Prince aux lys'' ou du ''Roi grand-prêtre''. Il est vêtu du pagne minoen et porte sur la tête une couronne de lys et de plumes de paon. Il tenait peut-être un animal sacré de la main gauche. Palais de Cnossos, fin du 15ème s. av. J.-C.

Η τοιχογραφία των Κρίνων, από την έπαυλη των κρίνων της Αμνισού.

The Lily fresco, from the Villa of the lilies at Amnissos.

Das Lilienfresko aus dem Lilienlandhaus in Amnissos.

La ''fresque des fleurs de lys''. Peinture murale provenant de la ''villa des fresques'' à Amnissos.

Το «Γαλάζιο πουλί». Από το σπίτι των τοιχογραφιών, στην Κνωσό, 15ος αιώνας π.Χ.

The Blue Bird. From the House of the Frescoes at Knossos, 15th century B.C.

Der ''Blaue Vogel''. Aus dem Freskenhaus in Knossos, 15. Jh. v. Chr.

''L' oiseau bleu''. Maison aux fresques, Cnossos, 15ème s. av. J.-C.

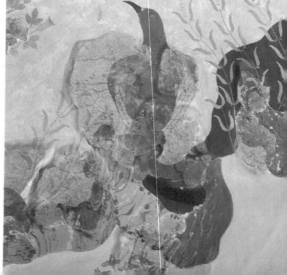

Ο περίφημος «ταυροκαθάπτης». Χρυσελεφάντινο ειδώλιο ταυρομάχου τη στιγμή που πηδά πάνω από τον ταύρο. Ανάκτορο Κνωσού. Γύρω στα 1500 π.Χ.

The famous "bull-leaper". A chrysselephantine figurine of a bull-leaper jumping over the bull. Palace at Knossos. About 1500 B.C.

Der berühmte "Stierkämpfer". Gold-elfenbeinernes Idol des Stierkämpfers in dem Augenblick, in dem er über den Stier springt. Palast von Knossos. Um 1500 v. Chr.

Le célèbre "acrobate au taureau". Statuette d' ivoire qui représente l' acrobate au moment où il saute au dessus du dos du taureau. Palais de Cnossos. 1500 av. J.-C environ.

Έξοχο ρυτό από ορεία κρύσταλλο. Το κρυστάλλινο δαχτυλίδι στη βάση του λαιμού στολίζεται με επίχρυσα φύλλα ελεφαντοστού. Οι χάντρες της λαβής συνδέθηκαν με μπρούτζινο σύρμα. Ανάκτορο Ζάκρου, 1500-1450 π.Χ.

Excellent rhyton of rock crystal. The crystal ring at the base of the neck is decorated with gilded ivory. The beads on the handle were connected by a bronze wire. Palace at Zakros. 1500-1450 B.C.

Hervorragendes rhyton aus Bergkristall. Der kristallene Ring an der Basis des Halses ist mit vergoldetem Elfenbein geschmiedet. Die Perlen des Henkels waren durch bronzenen Draht verbunden. Palast von Zakros. 1500-1450 v. Chr.

Splendide rhyton de cristal de roche. L' anneau de cristal qui entoure la base du col est orné de ivoire dorée. Les perles de l' anse sont retenues par un fil de bronze. Palais de Zakros, 1500-1450 av. J.-C.

Ο περίφημος «Δίσκος της Φαιστού». Στις δύο πλευρές του πήλινου δίσκου έχουν αποτυπωθεί —με κινητά στοιχεία— σε σπειροειδή διάταξη σύμβολα ιερογλυφικής γραφής που δεν έχει ακόμα αποκρυπτογραφηθεί. Γύρω στα 1600 π.Χ.

The famous «Phaestos Disk». Both sides of the clay disk have hieroglyphic characters separately impressed by means of punches and arranged in a spiral. The script has not yet been deciphered. About 1600 B.C.

Der berühmte «Diskus von Phästos». Auf beiden Seiten des Tondiskus sind in schneckenförmiger Anordnung durch bewegliche Lettern hieroglyphische Schriftsymbole aufgedruckt, die bis heute noch nicht entziffert sind. Um 1600 v. Chr.

Le célèbre «Disque de Phaistos». Les deux faces du disque de terre cuite portent des symboles d' écriture hiéroglyphique, disposés en spirale, qui n'ont pas encore été déchiffrés. 1600 av. J.-C. environ.

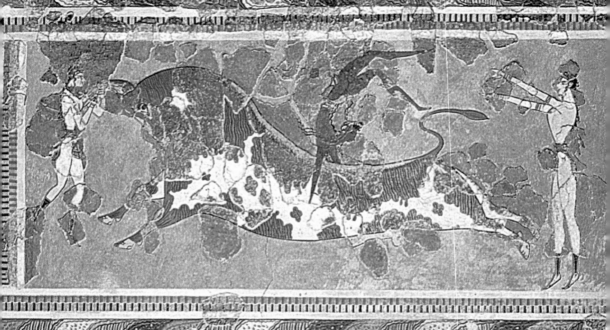

Οι «Γαλάζιες κυρίες», τοιχογραφία σε γαλάζιο βάθος. Είναι συμπληρωμένη σε πολλά μέρη με βάση άλλες τοιχογραφίες, αλλά είναι μια σπουδαία έκφραση της τέχνης της εποχής εκείνης. Τη χαριτωμένη στάση των χεριών ξαναβρίσκουμε μόνο στη τέχνη της Αναγέννησης. Βρέθηκε στην ανατολική πτέρυγα του ανακτόρου της Κνωσού. 15ος αι. π.Χ.

The "Ladies in Blue", a fresco with a blue background. It is restored in many places on the basis of other frescoes, but it is still an important example of the art of the period. The graceful posture of the arms is only found in the art of the Renaissance. It was discovered in the east wing of the palace of Knossos. 15th century B.C.

"Die Blauen Damen", Fresko auf blauem Untergrund. Es ist an vielen Stellen anhand anderer Fresken vervollständigt, aber es ist ein bedeutender Ausdruck der Kunst jener Epoche. Die graziöse Stellung der Hände finden wir nur in der Kunst der Renaissance wieder. Es wurde im Ostflügel des Palastes von Knossos gefunden. 15. Jh. v. Chr.

"Les dames en bleu". fresque sur fond bleu. Elle est en grande partie reconstituée, sur la base d' autres fresques, mais elle constitue un example important de l' expression artistique de cette époque. On ne retrouve ces gracieux mouvements des mains que dans l' art de la Renaissance. Elle a été découverte dans l' aile Est du palais de Cnossos. 15ème s. av. J.-C.

Η περίφημη τοιχογραφία των «Ταυροκαθαψίων». Προέρχεται από την ανατολική πτέρυγα του ανακτόρου της Κνωσού. Η παράσταση δείχνει το αγώνισμα στις διάφορες φάσεις του. Οι ταυροκαθάπτες είναι άνδρες και γυναίκες. 15ος αι. π.Χ.

The famous "Bull-leaping" fresco, from the East wing of the palace at Knossos. The different phases of the sport are shown. The bull-leapers are both men and women. 15th century B.C.

Das berühmte Fresko der "Stierspiele". Es stammt aus dem Ostflügel des Palastes von Knossos. Die Darstellung zeigt den Kampf in seinen verschiedenen Phasen. Die Stierkämpfer sind Männer und Frauen. 15. Jh. v. Chr.

La fameuse fresque du "jeu au taureau". Elle provient de l' aile Est du palais de Cnossos. La représentation montre les différentes phases du jeu, hommes et femmes qui sautent sur le dos d'un taureau. 15ème s. av. J.-C.

Θαυμάσιο τελετουργικό αγγείο από τη «δεξαμενή καθαρμών» της Ζάκρου. Μοναδικό για τη θαυμαστή αξιοποίηση των φλεβών και κηλίδων του χρωματιστού μαρμάρου και για την τολμηρότητα στο σχήμα του. 1500-1450 π.Χ.

Wonderful ritual vase from the "lustral basin" at Zakros. Unique for the marvellous use of the veins and spots in the coloured marble, and for its bold shape. 1500-1450 B.C.

Wundervolles Kultgefäß aus der "Lustralbechen" von Zakros. Einzigartig wegen der bewundernswerten Herausstellung der Adern und Flecken des farbigen Marmors und wegen der Kühnheit in seiner Form. 1500-1450 v. Chr.

Magnifique vase sacré du "bassin lustral" de Zakros. Il est unique par la mise en valeur des veines et des taches du marbre de couleur et par l' audacité de sa forme. 1500-1450 av. J.-C.

Το περίφημο ανάγλυφο «Ρυτό των θεριστών» από την Αγία Τριάδα. Είναι από στεατίτη και οι παραστάσεις του εικονίζουν πομπή ύστερα από τον θερισμό και το λίχνισμα. Ξεχωρίζει ομάδα μουσικών που τραγουδούν, ενώ ο πρώτος τους κρατά σείστρο. 16ος αι. π.Χ.

The famous "Rhyton of the Harvesters" from Ayia Triada. It is made of steatite and has scenes depicting a procession after the harvest and the winnowing. There is also a group of musicians singing, while the leader is holding a *seistrum* (rattle). 16th century B.C.

Das berühmte "Rhyton der Schnitter" aus Agia Triada. Es ist aus Steatit und seine Darstellungen zeigen eine Prozession nach dem Mähen und Korntrennen. Es unterscheidet sich eine Gruppe von Musikern, die singen, während der Erste von ihnen ein Sistrum hält. 16. jh. v. Chr.

Le fameux "rhyton aux moissonneurs" qui provient de Haghia Triada. Il est en stéatite et est orné d'un cortège d'hommes qui rentrent de la moisson et du battage du blé. Le groupe de musiciens qui chantent tandis que le premier d'entre eux tient un sistre, est particulièrement remarquable. 16ème s. av. J.-C.

Ρυτοφόροι, μέρος από την τοιχογραφία της πομπής. Ο ρυτοφόρος δίνει τον ιδεώδη τύπο της μινωικής νεολαίας με «δακτυλίδι μέση».

Cup-bearers, from the procession fresco. The cup-bearer depicted the ideal Minoan youth, with his slender waist.

Rhytonträger, ein Teil des Prozessionsfresko. Der Rhytonträger stellt den Idealtyp der minoischen Jugend dar, nämlich mit "ringschmaler Taille".

Les porteurs de vases. Fragment d'une peinture murale représentant une procession. Le porteur de rhyton est le type idéal de la jeunesse minoenne, caractérisée par la "taille de guêpe".

Περίφημο χρυσό κόσμημα από τον Χρυσόλακκο Μαλίων. Δυο μέλισσες απομυζούν μια σταγόνα μέλι. Έξοχο δείγμα της χρυσοχοϊκής τέχνης των Μινωιτών. Γύρω στα 1700 π.Χ.

Famous gold jewel from Chryssolakkos, Malia. Two bees are sucking a drop of honey. Excellent example of Minoan gold work. About 1700 B.C.

Berühmtes Goldschmuckstück aus «Chryssolakkos» von Malia. Zwei Bienen saugen einen Tropfen Honig auf. Vorzügliches Beispiel der Goldschmiedekunst der Minoer. Um 1700 v. Chr.

Fameux bijou en or de Chryssolakkos de Malia. Deux abeilles sucent une goutte de miel. C'est un example magnifique de l'orfèvrerie minoenne. Environs de 1700 av. J.-C.

Η περίφημη πέτρινη τοιχογραφημένη «σαρκοφάγος» της Αγίας Τριάδας, που έχει στις 4 πλευρές της παραστάσεις μινωικών νεκρικών τελετουργιών.

The famous stone "Ayia Triada Sarcophagus" which has frescoes portraying scenes of Minoan funeral ritual on all four sides.

Der berühmte steinerne, freskenverzierte "Sarkophag aus Agia Triada", der an seinen vier Seiten Darstellungen minoischer Totenzeremonien zeigt.

Le célèbre "sarcophage de Haghia Triada", peint sur les quatre côtés, avec des scènes de cérémonies funéraires minoennes.

Ο SIR ARTHUR EVANS, ανασκαφέας της Κνωσού (1851-1941).

SIR ARTHUR EVANS, the excavator of Knossos (1851-1941).

SIR ARTHUR EVANS (1851-1941), der die Ausgrabungen von Knossos durchführte.

SIR ARTHUR EVANS, qui a fait les fouilles de Cnossos (1851-1941).

ΚΝΩΣΟΣ - KNOSSOS

Γενική άποψη του ανακτόρου της Κνωσού. Το ανάκτορο της Κνωσού, όπως και τα άλλα ανάκτορα της μινωικής Κρήτης, αποτελούσε το πολιτικό, θρησκευτικό και οικονομικό κέντρο της περιοχής. Γύρω του απλωνόταν η πόλη της Κνωσού, που κατά τον Έβανς ξεπερνούσε με μέτριο υπολογισμό τους 100.000 κατοίκους. Το ανάκτορο είναι χτισμένο σε έκταση 22 χιλιάδων τ.μ. και ήταν πολυώροφο και πολυδαίδαλο. Στην Κνωσό βασίλεψε η δυναστεία του Μίνωα.

General view of the palace at Knossos. Like the other palaces of Minoan Crete, the palace at Knossos was the political, religious and economic centre of its region. The city of Knossos spread around it, with over 100,000 inhabitants at a conservative estimate, according to Evans. The palace covered an area of 22.000 square metres, was multi-storeyed and had an intricate plan. The dynasty of Minos ruled at Knossos.

Gesamtansicht des Palastes von Knossos. Der Palast von Knossos, wie auch die anderen Paläste des minoischen Kretas, bildeten das politische, religiöse und wirtschaftliche Zentrum des Gebietes. Um ihn breitete sich die Stadt von Knossos aus, die nach Evans mit mittlerer Schätzung 100.000 Einwohner übertraf. Der Palast ist auf einer Fläche 22.000 qm gebaut und war mehrstockwerkig und labyrinthartig. In Knossos herrschte die Dynastie des Minos.

Vue générale du palais de Cnossos. Le palais de Cnossos, comme tous les autres palais de l'époque minoenne, constituait le centre politique, religieux et économique de la région. Tout autour s'étendait la ville de Cnossos, qui, selon Evans, dépassait en tout cas 100.000 habitants. Le palais occupait une superficie de 22.000 m², sur plusieurs étages, avec un dédale de couloirs. C'est la dynastie de Minos qui régnait sur Cnossos.

Μέρος της νότιας πλευράς του ανακτόρου της Κνωσού με τα «ιερά κέρατα» και μεγάλους πίθους.
Part of the South side of the palace at Knossos, with the "sacred horns" and large pithoi.
Teil der Südseite des Palastes von Knossos mit den "Heiligen Hörnern" und den großen Fässern.
Vue partielle de la partie Sud du palais de Cnossos, avec les "cornes sacrées" et de grands pithos.

Κεντρικό κλιμακοστάσιο της Δ. πτέρυγας του Ανακτόρου.

The «Central Staircase» in the W. wing of the palace at Knossos.

Zentraltreppenhaus des Westflügels des Knossos-Palastes.

L' «escalier central» dans l'aile occidentale du palais de Cnossos.

Οι δυτικές αποθήκες του ανακτόρου της Κνωσού.

The west magazines of the palace at Knossos.

Die westlichen Vorratsräume des Palastes von Knossos.

Les magasins Ouest du palais de Cnossos.

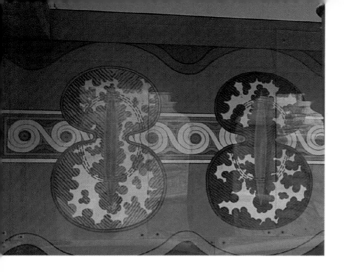

Το Μεγάλο Κλιμακοστάσιο στην Α. πτέρυγα
του ανακτόρου της Κνωσού.

The "Grand Staircase" in the E. wing of the
palace at Knossos.

Das große Treppenhaus im Ostflügel
des Knossos-Palastes.

Le "Grand escalier" dans l' aile orientale
du palais de Cnossos.

Ο περίφημος αλαβάστρινος θρόνος του Μίνωα, του βασιλιά-Αρχιερέα. Το θρόνο πλαισιώνουν γρύπες,
φανταστικά ιερά ζώα.

The famous alabaster throne of Minos, the priest-King. It is framed by griffins, which were imaginary
sacred animals.

Der berühmte Alabaster-Thron des Minos, Königs und Ober-priesters. Den Thron rahmen Greifen
phantastische heilige Tiere ein.

Le fameux trône d'albâtre de Minos, le roi grand-prêtre. Il est encadré de griffons, animaux légendaires
sacrés.

Μέρος της βόρειας εισόδου του ανακτόρου της Κνωσού, με την ανάγλυφη τοιχογραφία του ταύρου στην βεράντα του πυργίσκου ελέγχου.

Part of the north entrance of the palace at Knossos, with the relief fresco of the bull on the landing of the control bastion.

Teil des Nordeinganges des Palastes von Knossos mit dem reliefartigen Fresko des Stieres auf der Veranda des Kontrolturmes.

Vue partielle de l'entrée Nord du palais de Cnossos, avec la fresque en relief d'un taureau dans la véranda de la tourelle de surveillance.

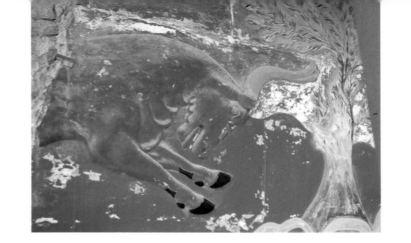

Το Μέγαρο της Βασίλισσας στην Α. πτέρυγα του ανακτόρου.
The Queen's megaron in the E. wing of the palace at Knossos.
Das Königin-Megaron im Ostflügel des Knossos-Palastes.
Le Mégaron de la reine. Aile orientale du palais de Cnossos.

Περίφημα Βυζαντινά κοσμήματα, (Ιστορικό Μουσείο Ηρακλείου).

Superb Byzantine jewellery, in the Historical Museum, Heraklion.

Berühmte Byzantinische Schmuckstücke (Historisches Museum von Heraklion).

Magnifiques bijoux Byzantins, du Musée Historique d'Héraklion.

Ο «Γιούχτας», το βουνό με τη μορφή ανθρώπινου προσώπου. Στην αρχαιότητα το θεωρούσαν ιερό, γιατί κατά την παράδοση εκεί θάφτηκε ο Δίας.

"Youktas", the mountain shaped like a human face. It was sacred in the ancient world because Zeus was buried there according to the tradition.

Der "Youktas", der Berg mit dem Aussehen eines menschlichen Gesichtes. In der Antike hielten sie ihn für heilig, weil dort nach der Überlieferung Zeus begraben war.

Le mont "Youkhtas", en forme de visage humain. Pendant l'antiquité, il était sacré, parce que la tradition disait que Zeus y avait été enterré.

Αρχαίο πατητήρι σταφυλιών στο Βαθύπετρο κοντά στις Αρχάνες.

Ancient wine press at Vathypetro near Archanes.

Alte Weintraubenkelter in Vathypetro.

Pressoir à vin, antique, à Vathypétro, prés d'Archanès.

ΦΑΙΣΤΟΣ - PFAESTOS

Γενική άποψη του ανακτόρου της Φαιστού. Δεσπόζει πάνω σε ακραίο λόφο του κάμπου της Μεσαράς. Η Φαιστός ήταν μια από τις αρχαιότερες και πιο σημαντικές κρητικές πόλεις. Από αρχαιολογική άποψη έρχεται αμέσως μετά την Κνωσό. Στη Φαιστό λέγεται ότι βασίλεψε η δυναστεία του Ραδάμανθυ.

General view of the palace at Phaestos. It stands on a hill at the edge of the Messara plain, which it dominates. Plaestos was one of the oldest and most important Cretan cities, and is second to Knossos in archaeological terms. The dynasty of Rhadamanthys is said to have ruled there.

Gesamtansicht des Palastes von Phästos. Er dominiert auf einem Randhügel der Messara-Ebene. Phästos war eine der ältesten und bedeutendsten kretischen Städte. Von archäologischer Sicht aus kommt Phästos direkt nach Knossos. In Phästos, sagt man, herrschte die Dynastie des Radamanthys.

Vue générale du palais de Phaistos. Il domine la plaine de la Messara, de l'une des collines qui l'entourent. Phaistos était l'une des plus anciennes et plus importantes villes de Crète. Elle vient juste après Cnossos du point de vue de l'intérêt archéologique. La légende veut que la dynastie de Radamantys régnait à Phaistos.

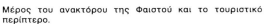

Μέρος του ανακτόρου της Φαιστού και το τουριστικό περίπτερο.

Part of the palace at Phaestos and the tourist pavilion.

Teilansicht des Palastes von Phästos und der Touristen-pavillon.

Vue partielle du palais de Phaistos, avec le pavillon touristique.

Άποψη της έπαυλης της Αγίας Τριάδας. Ίσως να αποτελούσε θερινή διαμονή των μελών της βασιλικής οικογένειας της Φαιστού.

View of the villa at Ayia Triada. It may have been the summer residence of the royal family at Phaestos.

Ansicht des Landhauses von Agia Triada. Vielleicht diente es als Sommeraufenthaltsort der Mitglieder der königlichen Familie von Phästos.

Vue de la villa de Haghia Triada. Il s' agissait peut-être de la résidence d'été de la famille royale de Phaistos.

Η κάρα του Αγίου Τίτου που φυλάσσεται στην ομώνυμη εκκλησία του Ηρακλείου.

The skull of St. Titus, which is kept in the church named after him in Heraklion.

Der Schädel des Agios Titus, der in der gleichnamigen Kirche von Heraklion aufbewahrt wird.

Le cràne de l'Apôtre Tite, conservé dans l'église qui lui est consacrée, à Héraclion.

Τα ερείπια της βυζαντινής εκκλησίας του Αποστόλου Τίτου, πρώτου επισκόπου της Κρήτης.

The ruins of the byzantine church of the Apostle Titus, first bishop of Crete.

Die Ruinen der byzantinischen Kirche des Apostel Titus, des ersten Bischofs von Kreta.

Les ruines de l'église byzantine de l'Apôtre Tite, premier évêque de Crète.

ΓΟΡΤΥΝΑ - GORTYS

Το Ωδείο και η στοά του, όπου εντοιχίστηκε η επιγραφή της νομοθεσίας. Η Γόρτυνα είναι από τις αρχαιότερες πόλεις της Κρήτης, έφτασε όμως στη μεγαλύτερη ακμή της στα ελληνορωμαϊκά χρόνια. Η παράδοση έλεγε πως πήρε το όνομά της από το γιο του Ραδάμανθυ Γόρτυνα. Η περίφημη επιγραφή είναι συγκεφαλαίωση νόμων κληρονομικού και οικογενειακού δικαίου και πολιτικής δικονομίας του 6ου π.Χ. αιώνα.

The theatre with stoa, where the law-code was inserted on the wall. Gortys was one of the most ancient cities in Crete, but reached the height of its prosperity during the Greco-Roman Period. According to tradition it was named after Gortys, the son of Rhadamanthys. The famous inscription is a summary of the laws relating to the rights of inheritance and of the family, and to the civil procedure of the 6th century B.C.

Das Theater und seine Stoa, wo die Inschrift der Gesetzgebung eingemauert war. Gortys ist eine der ältesten Städte Kretas, sie erreichte aber ihre größte Blütezeit in den griechisch-römischen Jahren. Die Überlieferung sagte, daß sie ihren Namen von dem Sohn des Radamanthys Gortys erhielt. Die berühmte Inschrift ist eine Gesetzeszusammenfassung des Erb-und Familienrechtes und der Zivilprozeßordnung des 6. Jh. v. Chr.

Le théâtre et son portique, dans un mur duquel était encastré l'inscription du code de Gortys. La ville est l'une des plus anciennes de Crète, mais son apogée ne remonte qu'à l'époque hellénistique et romaine. La légende dit qu'elle tient son nom de celui de Gortys, fils de Radamanthys. Le fameux code de Gortys est constitué par l'ensemble des lois du droit familial et du droit de succession, ainsi que de la procédure civile du 6ème s. an. J.-C.

Η ωραία ακτή Λέντα στα παράλια του Λιβυκού Πελάγους στο 20ο χλμ. από τη Φαιστό.

The beautiful beach Lenda, on the Libyan Sea 20 kms. from Phaestos.

Der schöne Strand von Lenda an der Küste des libyschen Meeres, 20 km von Phästos entfernt.

La merveilleuse baie de Lendas, sur la côte de la Mer Libyque.

Η περίφημη παραλία των Ματάλων με τα ταφικά της σπήλαια, στον κόλπο της Μεσαράς.

The famous coast of Matala in the gulf of Messara. The caves were used as tombs.

Der berühmte Strand von Matala mit seinen Grabhöhlen, in der Bucht von Messara.

La célèbre côte de Matala, dans le golfe de la Messara, avec ses grottes et sa plage.

Το χωριό Πρινιάς Μαλεβιζίου. Σε ψηλό γειτονικό λόφο βρισκόταν η αρχαία πόλη «Ριζηνία», από την οποία διατηρήθηκαν πολύ σημαντικά κτίρια και τάφοι.

The village of Prinias, Malevizi. The ancient city of "Rhizenia" was on a neighbouring hill; buildings and tombs of great importance survive.

Das Dorf Prinias (Malevisi). Auf dem hohen benachbarten Hügel befand sich die antike Stadt "Risinia", von der sehr bedeutende Gebäude und Gräber erhalten sind.

Le village de Prinias de Malevizi. Sur une haute colline, tout près delà, se trouvait la ville antique de Rhizinia, dont subsistent des constructions importantes, ainsi que des tombes.

Παραλία της Αγ. Πελαγίας, δυτικά από το Ηράκλειο.

The coast at Ayia Pelayia, to the West of Heraklion.

Der Strand von Agia Pelagia, westlich von Heraklion.

La côte d'Haghia Pelagia, à l'Ouest d' Héraclion.

Το χωριό Φόδελε, που μερικοί το θεώρησαν ιδιαίτερη πατρίδα του διάσημου ζωγράφου Δομήνικου Θεοτοκόπουλου (El-Greco) και η προτομή του.

The village of Fodele, and the bust of the famous painter Domenikos Theotokopoulos (El-Greco). The village is thought by many to have been his home.

Das Dorf Fodele, das mehrere für den Geburtsort des berühmten Malers Domenikos Theotokopoulos (El-Greco) halten und seine Büste.

Le village de Fodèlè, qu'on a quelque fois dit être le lieu d'origine du célèbre peintre Domenicos Theotokopoulos (El-Greco), et son buste.

Σταλίδα. Χώρος παραθερισμού όχι μακριά από τα Μάλια.

Stalis, a summer resort not far from Malia.

Stalida. Urlaubsort, nicht weit von Malia.

Stalida, lieu de vacances, non loin de Malia.

Η παραλία των Μαλίων, όχι μακριά από το ανάκτορο.

The coast of Malia, not far from the Minoan palace.

Der Strand von Malia, nicht weit von dem minoischen Palast entfernt.

La plage de Malia, non loin du palais minoen.

ΜΑΛΙΑ - MALIA

Ανάκτορο Μαλίων. Μέρος της πτέρυγας των ιερών με την ιδιόρ-ρυθμη τράπεζα προσφορών. Το ανάκτορο ήταν ανάλογο με εκείνα της Κνωσού και της Φαιστού. Στα Μάλια πιστεύεται ότι βασίλεψε η δυναστεία του Σαρπηδόνα.

The palace at Malia. Part of the wing of the sanctuaries, with the unusual offering table. The palace was like those at Knossos and Phaestos. The dynasty of Sarpedon is thought to have ruled at Malia.

Der Palast von Malia. Teil des Flügels des Heiligtums mit dem eigentümlichen Opfertisch. Der Palast war ähnlich denen von Knos-sos und Phästos. Man glaubt, daß in Malia die Dynastie des Sarpedon herrschte.

Le palais de Malia. Partie de l'aile des sanctuaires, avec une table à offrandes très particulière. Le palais était du même type que ceux de Cnossos et de Phaistos. On croit que c'est la dynastie de Sarpédon qui y régnait.

Μάλια. Μινωικό πιθάρι των παλαιοανακτορικών χρόνων με γιγάντιες διαστάσεις.

Malia. Giant Minoan pithos from the first palace period.

Malia: minoisches Faß der älteren Palastzeit mit gigantischen Ausmaßen.

Malia. Pithos minoen géant, de l'époque protopalatiale.

Χερσόνησος: Στη θέση της ομώνυμης αρχαίας πόλης, λιμανιού της Λύκτου.

Chersonessos, on the site of the ancient city of that name, the harbour of Lyktos.

Chersonissos. An Stelle der alten gleichnamigen Stadt, des Hafens der Lyktos.

Chersonissos. La ville moderne se trouve sur l'emplacement de la ville antique du même nom, qui était le port de Lyctos.

Το φημισμένο οροπέδιο του Λασιθίου, με τους 10.000 ανεμόμυλους. Υγιεινός και θαυμάσιος τόπος παραθερισμού.

The famous plain of Lassithi, with its 10.000 windmills. A wonderfully healthy summer retreat.

Die berühmte Hochebene von Lassithi mit ihren 10.000 Windmühlen. Gesunde und wundervolle Gegend für sommerferien.

La fameuse plaine de Lassithi, avec ses 10.000 moulins à vent. C'est un magnifique lieu de séjour, extrêmement salubre.

ΝΕΑΠΟΛΗ - NEAPOLIS

Η Νεάπολη από τις σπουδαιότερες και γραφικότερες κωμοπόλεις του νομού Λασιθίου.

Neapolis, one of the most important and attractive villages in the *nomos* of Lassithi.

Neapoli, Eine der bedeutendsten und malerischsten Städtchen des Lassithi-Bezirkes.

Néapoli, l'une des plus importantes et des plus jolies bourgades du département de Lassithi.

ΑΓΙΟΣ ΝΙΚΟΛΑΟΣ - AGIOS NIKOLAOS

Ο Άγιος Νικόλαος με τη λίμνη. Πρωτεύουσα του νομού Λασιθίου, με πληθυσμό 8.000 κατοίκους περίπου. Από τα γνωστότερα τουριστικά κέντρα της Κρήτης.

The harbour of Ayios Nikolaos, administrative capital of the *nomos* of Lassithi, with about 8.000 inhabitants. It is one of the best known tourist centres in Crete.

Agios Nikolaos mit dem See. Hauptstadt des Bezirkes von Lassithi mit einer Bevölkerung von ungefähr 8.000 Einwohnern. Eines der bekanntesten Touristenzentren Kretas.

Haghios Nicolaos, avec son lac. C'est le chef-lieu du département de Lassithi; la ville compte 8.000 habitants environ, et constitue l'un des centres touristiques les mieux connus de Crète.

Τοιχογραφία της Παναγίας της Κεράς.

Fresco from the Panayia Keras.

Fresko der «Panajia i Kera».

Fresque de l'église de la Vierge Kéra.

Κριτσά. Η Παναγία της Κεράς, με πολύ σημαντικές τοιχογραφίες. Είναι από τις πιο καλά διατηρημένες βυζαντινές
εκκλησίες της Κρήτης και χρονολογείται στον 13ο αιώνα.

Kritsa. The Panayia Kera, with its important frescoes. This is
one of the best preserved Byzantine churches in Crete. It
dates from the 13th century.

Kritsa. Die Kirche Panajia i Kera (Mutter Gottes die Herrin)
mit vielen bedeutenden Fresken. Sie ist eine der besterhalte-
nen byzantinischen Kirchen Kretas und datiert aus dem
13.Jh.

Kritsa. L'église de la Vierge Kéra, avec de très importantes
fresques. C'est l'une des mieux conservées des églises
byzantines de Crète; elle date du XIIIè s.

Μαγευτική τοποθεσία στην Ελούντα, όπου
η αρχαία πόλη Ολούς.

Enchanting countryside at Elounda, site of
the ancient city of Olous.

Zauberhafte Gegend in Elounda, dort, wo
sich die antike Stadt Olous befand.

Magnifique paysage à Elounda, où se
dressait l' ancienne Olous.

ΓΟΥΡΝΙΑ - GOURNIA

Γενική άποψη της μινωικής πόλης Γουρνιά. Στη θέση Γουρνιά ανασκάφτηκε μεγάλος μινωικός οικισμός με βιοτεχνικό, αγροτικό και ψαράδικο χαρακτήρα, που ήταν σε ακμή γύρω στα 1600 π.Χ. Δίνει την καλύτερη εικόνα για τις προϊστορικές πόλεις της Κρήτης.

General view of the town of Gournia. A large Minoan settlement has been excavated at Gournia, where industry, farming and fishing were practised, and which reached the height of its prosperity about 1600 B.C. It gives the best picture we have of a Cretan prehistoric town.

Gesamtansicht der Stadt von Gournia. In Gournia wurde eine große minoische Siedlung mit handwerklichem, landwirtschaftlichem und Fischerei-Charakter ausgegraben, welche ihre Blütezeit um 1600 v. Chr. hatte. Sie gibt das beste Bild für die prehistorischen Städte Kretas.

Vue générale de la ville de Gournia. A cet endroit, on a dégagé un grand centre minoen, à la fois artisanal et agricole, et également centre de pêche. Il a connu son apogée vers 1600 av. J.-C. Gournia donne la meilleure idée de ce que devaient être les villes préhistoriques de Crète.

ΙΕΡΑΠΕΤΡΑ - IERAPETRA

Η Ιεράπετρα στη νότια παραλία της Κρήτης με την θαυμάσια παραλία της και τα ψαροκάϊκά της.

Ierapetra on the South coast of Crete, with its wonderful beach, and fishing boats.

Hierapetra an der Südküste Kretas mit seinem wundervollen Strand und seinen Fischerbooten.

Hiérapétra, sur la côte Sud de la Crète, avec sa magnifique plage et ses caiques de pêcheurs.

ΣΗΤΕΙΑ - SITIA

Η γραφική Σητεία, στην ανατολική Κρήτη. Είναι χτισμένη αμφιθεατρικά σε χαμηλό λόφο και έχει θαυμάσιο κλίμα.

The picturesque town of Sitia, in east Crete. It is al amphitheatrically built on a low hill, and has a superb climate.

Das malerische Sitia in Ostkreta. Es ist amphitheatrisch auf einem niedrigen Hügel erbaut und hat ein wundervolles Klima.

La pittoresque ville de Sitia, en Créte orientale. Elle est construite en amphithéâtre sur une basse colline, et jouit d'un excellent climat.

Βάι. Το γνωστό φοινικόδασος με τις 5.000 περίπου φοινικιές στην ανατολική παραλία της Κρήτης.

Vaï. The famous palm forest, with about 5.000 palm trees, on the East coast of Crete.

Vai. Der bekannte Palmenwald mit den ungefähr 5.000 Palmen an der Ostküste Kretas.

Vaï. La fameuse forêt de palmiers, 5.000 arbres environs, sur la côte orientale de Crète.

ΑΝΑΚΤΟΡΟ ΖΑΚΡΟΥ
PALACE OF ZAKROS

Άποψη του ανακτόρου της Κάτω Ζάκρου. Η θέση του στην ανατολική άκρη του νησιού ευνοούσε τις εμπορικές επαφές με την Αίγυπτο και την Ανατολή. Το νέο παλάτι χτίστηκε γύρω στα 1600 π.Χ.

View of the palace at Kato Zakros. Its position on the East coast of the island, favoured commercial contacts with Egypt and the East. The second palace was built about 1600 B.C.

Ansicht des Palastes von Kato Zakros. Seine Lage am Ostende der Insel begünstigte die Handelsbeziehungen mit Ägypten und Aħatolien. Der neue Palast wurde um 1600 v. Chr erbaut.

Vue du palais de Kato Zakros. Sa situation géographique, à l'extrêmité Est de l'île, favorisait les transactions commerciales avec l'Egypte et l'Orient. Le nouveau palais a été construit aux environs de 1600 av. J.-C.

Σταφύλια «ροζακί».

«Rozaki» grapes.

Weintrauben «Rosaki».

Raisins «Rosaki».

ΑΓΡΟΤΙΚΗ ΖΩΗ - RUSTIC LIFE
ΑΡΧΑΝΕΣ - ARCHANES

Η κωμόπολη Αρχάνες στα νότια του Ηρακλείου, το μεγαλύτερο κέντρο παραγωγής των περίφημων επιτραπέζιων σταφυλιών του είδους «ροζακί» που θεωρούνται η καλύτερη ποικιλία σταφυλιών του κόσμου.

The village of Archanes, south of Heraklion, is the biggest producer of the famous "Rozaki" grapes, which are thought to be the best in the world.

Das Städtchen Archanes im Süden von Heraklion, das größte Produktionszentrum der berühmten Tafeltrauben der Sorte "Rosaki", die für die beste Weintraubenauswahl der Welt gehalten wird.

La bourgade d' Archanès, au Sud d'Héraclion. C'est le plus grand centre de production des fameux raisins de type "rosaki", qui est considérée comme la meilleure variété de raisin du monde.

Τρύγος σταφυλιών. Ο τρύγος στην Κρήτη αρχίζει στις αρχές του Σεπτέμβρη και παίρνει το χαρακτήρα αγροτικού λαϊκού πανηγυριού. Το κρασί θεωρούνταν και θεωρείται πάντα πολύτιμο, ιερό ποτό.

Harvesting the grapes. The grape harvest, which starts at the beginning of September in Crete, has the air of a popular rural festival. Wine was, and is, considered to be very precious, with an almost sacred character.

Die Weinlese. Die Weinlese beginnt auf Kreta Anfang September und nimmt den Charakter eines ländlichen Volksrestes an. Man hielt den Wein — und er wird immer noch — für ein wertvolles, fast heiliges Getränk gehalten.

La Vendange. En Grète, les vendanges commencent au début de Septembre et constituent une fête populaire. Le vin a toujours été considéré comme une boisson précieuse, presque sacrée .

Τύπος κρητικού βοσκού.

Cretan shepherd.

Typischer kretischer Hirt.

Type de berger crétois.